Dedicated to my parents and my family
for their love and support.

UNDERSTANDING EMPLOYEE
INFORMATION BEHAVIOR

ⓒ Seok Noh Ph.D., 2024

초판 1쇄 발행 2024년 8월 16일

지은이   Seok Noh Ph.D.
펴낸이   이기봉
편집   좋은땅 편집팀
펴낸곳   도서출판 좋은땅
주소   서울특별시 마포구 양화로12길 26 지월드빌딩 (서교동 395-7)
전화   02)374-8616~7
팩스   02)374-8614
이메일   gworldbook@naver.com
홈페이지   www.g-world.co.kr

ISBN   979-11-388-3435-3 (03320)

DOCTORAL DISSERTATION WRITING PROCESS

UNDERSTANDING EMPLOYEE INFORMATION BEHAVIOR

Focusing on China's Small and Medium-sized Enterprises (SMEs)

Seok Noh Ph.D.

좋은땅

Foreword

In a society full of information, people are facing a problem of how to pick, digest and get useful information. The same goes true with enterprises.

Enterprises can be divided into large, medium, small and micro ones. The medium and small enterprises are typical ones according to their sizes. In this book, they are referred to as small and medium-sized enterprises (SMEs). SMEs have a larger scale of production relative to micro-enterprises, for example, a higher degree of concentration of labor force, means of labor, objects of labor and production. They play an important role in the economy and are the focus of national construction. With the socialization of production and scientific and technological progress, SMEs bring obvious economic benefits in terms of investment as well as production and operation. As important carriers for mass entrepreneurship and innovation, they have an irreplaceable role in lifting employment, economic growth, scientific and technological innovation and social harmony and stability. Thus, they are of strategic significance to the national economy and social development. The essence of SMEs is development while the core of development is performance. In this case, the performance of SMEs is particularly important. That is to say, improving the enterprise performance is an everlasting task.

By referring to relevant literature, it is understood that many factors affect enterprise performance. For example, internal management, internal and external environment, enterprise managers and employees. This book is a reference book specially written for analyzing the performance and planning the development of Chinese SMEs. It also includes how to improve the performance of localized SMEs by combining the characteristics of Chinese SMEs while based on the expectation theory and the Chinese relational culture. Moreover, this book introduces the basic theories and knowledge points related to employees' information contribution, performance expectations and relational expectations. Besides these, it also gives a theoretical model of expectation theory, and carries out data analysis and structural equation validation of the model's reliability and operability, stressing the importance of combining the theoretical design of the model with the practicalities of Chinese SMEs environment.

Understanding Employee Information Behavior consists of 6

chapters. Chapter 1 includes a brief review and introduction of the purpose and background of this research and puts forward related questions. In Chapter 2, a theoretical review is given, detailing the factors influencing information contribution, as well as the effects of relationship culture and employee performance expectations on information contribution with Chinese characteristics. Chapter 3 shows a structural model for modeling and simulation of information contribution. Chapter 4 gives a careful description of the research methodology, including questionnaire research, variable definitions, etc. Chapter 5 is about data analysis, which further validates the stability and operability of the model through SPSS&AMOS data software analysis. Chapter 6 concludes with implications, limitations and future research.

This book is revised and perfected on the basis of my doctoral dissertation, which systematically shows the framework and process of enterprise case study. It is of help to the readers' practical dissertation writing and statistical analysis of data. Moreover, it is an attempt to combine the basic theory with Chinese relational culture. By reading it, readers are hoped to have a deep understanding of China and Chinese SMEs or get partial references and guidelines as SMEs operators.

For the data analysis of this book, please refer to Dr. Bridge's WeChat Official Account of academic research. In view of the limitations, errors are inevitable, so we are open to readers' comments and corrections.

Author Seok Noh.

June, 2024

CONTENTS

Chapter 6 *125*

VI. Conclusions *125*

List of Figures

List of Tables

Chapter 1

I. Introduction

The performance of an enterprise is the core of its development. In this development, the factors of knowledge and information especially influence enterprise performance. Knowledge and information can not only improve the competitiveness of enterprise organizations, but also enhance their added value. In turn, there are many other factors that also affect the sharing of knowledge and information. The influence of, for example, personal, organizational, and environmental factors is characterized by a certain randomness, and may limit the performance of enterprises and organizations. To overcome this problem and improve the value of knowledge and information for enterprises, I conduct in-depth research on information contribution and explore which factors influence employee information contribution.

Information contribution constitutes the early stage of information sharing. Only when employees have the motivation to contribute information or have expectations after contributing information will they work hard to contribute their own information, and thus create additional value for and enhance the competitiveness of the enterprise.

Knowledge and information have evolved to be important sources of competitive advantage; they are fundamental drivers of business success (Bock et al. 2007). Indeed, organizations that facilitate knowledge exchange benefit from long-term competitive advantages (Barua et al. 2007; Wagner 2006). We also know that employees are more productive if they engage in beneficial information-sharing behaviors (Baird and Henderson 2001; Teece 2000). Thus, improving the organizational efficiency and organizational performance of small and medium-sized enterprises (SMEs) is foundational to research on such organizations. When employees facilitate information sharing, organizations can increase information flow, efficiency, and effectiveness, and respond more quickly to changing customer needs. However, contextual factors, such as the type of industry, size of organization, and type of organizational structure, may affect the quality of the information provided (Li and Lin 2006).

This research explores the influencing factors of information contribution within SMEs from the perspective of knowledge and information. The sharing of knowledge and information not only affects employee productivity and work relationships within an organization, but is also known to affect organizational performance. While it is generally accepted that the value of knowledge largely determines the fate of an organization (Grant 1996), the question posed by Wasko and Faraj (2005) received widespread attention from scholars and practitioners 17 years ago (Hwang et al. 2015; Wang et al. 2014).

Organizations are now more committed to discovering and leveraging knowledge-based resources. A key aspect of this effort is encouraging employees to contribute their knowledge and information through a variety of channels, such as face-to-face communication, email, online chat, and online discussions. The critical role of personal knowledge and information, especially in improving organizational performance, ranges from avoiding mistakes to initiating organizational progress (Blatt et al. 2006; Liu et al. 2014). However, personal knowledge is often considered to be highly private and a source of personal superiority over others (Ipe 2003; Lin and Huang 2010). That is, knowledge and information contributions benefit the organization at the expense of individual advantages (Yu and Chu 2007). However, reciprocal communication is essential to efficiency of work among employees and to increase organizational productivity (Blau 1963; Flynn 2003a). One of the benefits of reciprocal exchanges is better cooperation among employees (Emerson 1976). When employees provide valuable information to the organization, both organizational work efficiency and performance improve; in return, the organization offers feedback to employees through corresponding incentives and compensation, creating a virtuous cycle of increasing information contribution and greater incentives and compensation.

A knowledge-based view of the firm (Grant 1991, 1996; Spender 1996; Teece 2000) holds that knowledge is the foundation of a firm's competitive advantage and, ultimately, a major driver of firm value. However, knowledge and information exist inherently within individuals (Nonaka and Konno 1998) and, more specifically, within employees who create, identify, archive, access, and apply knowledge to perform tasks. Thus, the movement of knowledge and information across personal and organizational boundaries, in and out of repositories, and into organizational routines and practices ultimately depends on the information-contribution behavior of employees. When the information contribution of the entire organization is limited, the potential for information gaps increases, which can lead to suboptimal work outcomes (Baird and Henderson 2001).

Work engagement has a large and positive effect on an employee's intention to share knowledge (Song et al. 2014; Chen et al. 2011;

Tang et al. 2015). Employees who are engaged in and enthusiastic about their work are more likely to share job-related ideas and expertise with their coworkers (Chen et al. 2011) because knowledge sharing is a self-motivated and proactive habit. The same can be said of the positive influence of employee job satisfaction on innovative work behavior (Agarwal 2014; Agarwal et al. 2012; De Spiegelaere et al. 2016). In this study, I investigate the mediating effect of work engagement.

In addition to the above background factors, I also introduce the relationship factor because the survey sample constitutes employees of SMEs in China. A relationship is the fundamental link between today's Chinese enterprises and the Chinese people that maintains economic and social activities. A relationship generally refers to a social relationship based in mutual benefit; it is a special social relationship that helps maintain partners in a mutually beneficial manner through mutual responsibility for resource acquisition and ongoing cooperation. In China, more emphasis is placed on *guanxi* exchanges, and Chinese companies and Chinese people attach more importance to *guanxi* to conduct economic transactions and maintain social contacts. Noh (2022) claims that interrelationships can be improved through knowledge sharing, and that employees operating on aspirations may have positive attitudes toward information sharing out of an interest in fairness and reciprocity.

Noh and Kang (2021) further state that the motivation for obtaining personal information is to maintain relationships or friendships. These findings suggest that Chinese respondents place greater emphasis on friendship, which highlights the characteristics of Chinese relationship culture.

The goal of this study is to gain a better understanding of the factors that influence the proclivity of employees in Chinese SMEs to engage in information contribution behaviors. Because such behavior can be influenced not only by individual motivations but also by situational forces (Yoo and Torrey 2002), and there already exists extensive literature on the associations between performance expectation, relationship expectation, work engagement, and information contribution (Huber 2001; Lee et al. 2020; Bock et al. 2005), I employ a theoretical framework that incorporates expectancy theory.

I extend the definition of performance expectation through the study of expectancy theory. I show that performance expectation can motivate employees to contribute to information. Owing to the relational nature of culture among Chinese SMEs, I emphasize the importance of relationship expectation, focusing on its role in employee information contribution. Additionally, the results— that employees who are engaged and enthusiastic about their work are more likely to contribute work-related information to their colleagues—are corroborated. The study also found that work engagement and performance expectation, relationship expectation, and information contribution intention behavior are closely related. Performance and relationship expectations affect information contribution through the mediating influence of work engagement, and, similarly, the effect of relationship expectation is strengthened through the mediation of work engagement. While studies have focused on personal cognition or social networks, I examine the combined effects of performance expectation, relationship expectation, and work engagement on organizational information contribution. Finally, by illustrating the various roles of relationship and performance expectations in organizations, and the mediating role of work engagement, this study contributes to the long-term development of the entire organization. While sharing such information may be beneficial to other members of the organization, it does require the information provider to devote a certain amount of time and effort to share such information. In most organizations, more people consume information than contribute to it. Although these organizations thrive as people provide autonomous information, there is limited research on the factors that influence people's willingness to provide information, and multiple factors may be at play.

This study deals with employee information contribution within an organization, and I specifically focus on the organization of Chinese SMEs. The research questions are set up as follows:

1) What is the role of information contribution in SMEs?

2) What factors affect employee information contribution behavior?

3) Which factors mediate the effect of employee information contribution behavior?

Beginning with these questions, I design the theoretical basis and study variables, and develop models and hypotheses through a theoretical review and framework. The remaining study is organized as follows. The following section examines important literature on expectancy theory, information contribution behavior, as well as some motivational debates related to them, before developing study hypotheses based on regulatory focus theory. Survey research experimental data are used to examine hypothetical models to answer the research question. Finally, the findings are addressed as well as their ramifications.

Chapter 2

II. Theoretical Review

Literature research requires a critical reading of literature resources using the keywords of definitions of information, knowledge, and knowledge sharing; information contribution; information contribution influencing factors (personal factors such as intrinsic motivation, extrinsic motivation, and personal trust; organizational factors such as organizational trust, organizational culture, national culture, shared culture, and organizational citizen behavior; and technical factors); expectancy theory; China's relationship culture; relationship networks and knowledge sharing; work engagement; and information contribution. The following discussion will focus on the definitions of concepts and how they fit into expectancy theory.

2.1 Information, Knowledge, and Knowledge Sharing

Despite the many attempts to define "information" and "knowledge" there remains a lack of a clear and complete description of what they are and how they are related. Although many definitions are related, they are far from complete. The definitions of information and knowledge are organized as follows:

Information

A message containing relevant meaning, implication, or input for a decision and/or action is referred to as information. Current (communication) and historical (processed data or reconstructed image) sources are used to gather information data. In essence, the goal of information is to assist in making decisions, solving issues, or seizing opportunities.

Knowledge

Our understanding of knowledge can be thought of as the know-what, know-how, and know-why capacity that resides in the human mind. Everyone learns and increases knowledge in order to improve their lives; however, the goal of business knowledge is to create or add value to organizations, including companies, and all their stakeholders. Liew (2007) holds that the ultimate goal of knowledge is to create value.

According to the knowledge-based view of companies (Grant 1991, 1996; Spender 1996; Teece 2000), knowledge is the cornerstone and foundation of a company's competitive advantage, and, ultimately, becomes the core driver of company value.

Knowledge Sharing

The way knowledge is shared within an organization is the core issue of knowledge management; it is considered to be the company's most valuable resource (Grant 1996). Knowledge sharing, according to Hendriks (1999), entails a relationship between at least two parties: one who holds the knowledge and the other who receives it. Individuals in organizations have always created and exchanged knowledge; hence, knowledge sharing was seen to be a naturally occurring activity. Knowledge sharing is a dynamic process influenced by a variety of complicated elements at the corporate, group, and individual levels (Andrews and Delahaye 2000; Davenport and Prusak 1998).

Individuals have inherent knowledge—this is particularly true for employees who generate, identify, document, access, and apply knowledge while performing tasks (Nonaka and Konno 1998). Thus, the information-sharing activities of employees are ultimately responsible for the movement of knowledge across personal and organizational boundaries, in and out of repositories, and into organizational routines and practices. When knowledge exchange within an organization is restricted, the risk of knowledge gaps grows, and these gaps are more likely to result in less-than-ideal work outcomes (Baird and Henderson 2001).

Associating knowledge with power makes it extremely difficult to share knowledge within an organization. To solve this problem and dilemma, we must provide numerous incentives to encourage people to share with others the information and knowledge they possess. O'Reilly and Pondy (1980) surmise a strong correlation between individual rewards and knowledge-sharing behaviors. Gupta and Govindarajan's (2000) case study illustrates that significant changes in incentive systems are required to encourage individuals to share their knowledge and information, particularly in an internal technology network-based organization.

Definitions of information and knowledge, and the relationship between information and knowledge, are often considered interchangeable, or can be considered related with intended applications. If you accept and internalize external information, it becomes knowledge; and if you externalize knowledge that you know, it becomes information again.

For example, in an organization, information is transformed into knowledge if an employee accepts information contributed by other employees and applies it to the internal organization. Employees again contribute knowledge to other employees, and this knowledge is transformed back into information. Such is the cyclic process of knowledge and information exchange. In this study, I use the concepts of information and knowledge interchangeably.

2.2 Limitations of Knowledge Sharing

Although information and knowledge can be used as interchangeable concepts, they are still conceptually different. In this study, information can be understood as the content that helps companies make decisions, solve problems, and seize opportunities. There are also essential differences between information contribution and knowledge sharing. I thus summarize the characteristics and limitations of knowledge sharing as follows:

First, the knowledge-sharing activities of employees are influenced by personal and intra-organizational communication; when knowledge and information exchange within an organization is limited, the risk of knowledge gaps increases, and these gaps are more likely to lead to less-than-ideal work outcomes (Baird and Henderson 2001).

Second, a variety of complex factors at the organizational and individual levels affect the dynamic process of knowledge sharing (Andrews and Delahaye 2000; Davenport and Prusak 1998). Sharing knowledge within an organization requires us to provide many incentives to encourage employees to share the information and knowledge they have, all of which limit employee knowledge sharing.

Finally, according to Hendriks (1999), knowledge sharing requires a relationship between at least two parties: one party holds knowledge, and the other party receives it. Individuals in an organization always create and exchange knowledge, which makes knowledge sharing a naturally occurring activity that is not affected by time and environment, has no clear purpose, and does not motivate employees to share knowledge.

Based on these limitations of knowledge sharing, I focus on information contribution within the organization, posing the following questions: what is information contribution and what are the characteristics of information contribution?

2.3 What is Information Contribution?

Information contribution behavior is a manifestation of employees' own internal motivation; it is also the early stage of information sharing. Only when employees have the motivation to contribute information or have expected results after contributing information will they make efforts to contribute their own information, create added value for the enterprise, and enhance the competitiveness of the enterprise.

Information behavior refers to the purposeful participation of users in the retrieval, adoption, and dissemination of information; content creation and sharing; and other activities. In this section, I review and organize the relevant literature on information sharing and information contribution. I document and explain the content of information contribution among individuals within a network as well as information contribution among members of the organization.

Let us first consider individual information sharing on the Internet. Individual information sharing—also called information donation in the information-sharing process—refers to individuals providing their information (Wang and Noe 2010). It takes place in both physical and virtual communities, and it takes place through a variety of means such as face-to-face conversation, email, online chat, and online discussion (Ray et al. 2014; Liu et al. 2014; Ma and Agarwal 2007; Wasko and Faraj 2005). Information is often regarded as very private, or even the source of individual status vis-à-vis others, as Ipe (2003) points out. This means individuals who are not highly motivated may not contribute (Lin and Huang 2010); that is, knowledge sharing can never be imposed, only prompted.

Next, let us consider information sharing among organizational members. Information sharing among employees is represented by efforts and contributions to the creation of an organizational knowledge database, and it has piqued the interest of practitioners and researchers (Cabrera and Cabrera 2002; Hansen 2002).

Knowledge sharing within a firm is a critical issue in knowledge management, and it is regarded as a firm's most valuable resource because it embodies intangible assets and creative processes that are difficult to replicate (Grant 1996; Porter and Liebeskind 1996). This reciprocal interchange is vital in molding employees' perceptions of one another and enhancing the productivity of firms (Blau 1963; Flynn 2003a). Note that most discussions of knowledge management and information sharing differentiate between data, information, and knowledge.

One of the gains of reciprocal exchange is cooperation (Emerson 1976). Employees can also gain valuable resources, such as expertise and information content, over time by giving and receiving benefits—not because of hierarchical power or contractual obligations, but because the rules of reciprocity are so strongly supported by each other (Flynn 2003b; Heath 1976).

Information exchange is a critical component for firms striving to stay competitive (Moberg et al. 2002), and understanding and putting information sharing into practice are seen as critical for businesses to be competitive and profitable. Successful exchanges require a free flow of information, which refers to the movement of information or data among members of an organization.

Workers will be more productive if they develop favorable information-sharing behaviors (Baird and Henderson 2001; Teece

2000). When information sharing is promoted, a company can increase information flow, efficiency, and effectiveness, as well as respond to changing customer needs more quickly. Organizations that foster knowledge exchange do gain long-term competitive advantages (Barua et al. 2007; Wagner 2006) because knowledge is a known driver of business success (Bock et al. 2007). This relationship is further altered by contextual factors, such as the type of industry, size of the organization, and type of organizational structure, that affect the quality of information provided (Li and Lin 2006).

Individuals who generate, recognize, archive, access, and utilize information when performing their activities possess useful information and expertise (Grant 1996; Nonaka and Konno 1998). The information sharing activities of employees determine how information moves across individual and organizational boundaries into organizational routines and practices. Information gaps are more likely to occur when there is a lack of information sharing across an organization (Baird and Henderson 2001; Teece 2000). Within organizations, information is usually exchanged through networks of members (Barua et al. 2007; Hatala 2006). In fact, members with higher-strength networks are more likely to obtain higher-quality information than those with lower-strength networks (Parker et al. 2001; Sinkula 1994).

The behavioral intentions of individuals toward information

sharing and contribution in the network is a popular subject of study. In this study, I focus on information contribution content in the context of the behavioral intentions of employees in the organization. That is, what are the factors in an organization that affect employee information contribution?

2.4 Influencing Factors of Information Contribution

The literature has long identified a wide range of factors that influence employees' knowledge- and information-sharing behaviors across various industries and types of organizations. The streams of research on factors affecting information contribution can be classified into three broad factors: situational and context, relationship, and knowledge.

Situational and context factors indicate the characteristics of an organization, such as organizational culture, leadership, organizational structure, information technology, and compensation system. Relationship factors are components that facilitate the relationship among groups or organizations that transmit and accept knowledge, and include trust level, communication level, intimacy, mutual influence, characteristics of recipients, characteristics of beneficiaries, information on knowledge holders, and competitive relationships among groups. The knowledge factors are related to which attributes are shared, and include whether the knowledge can be codified, causal ambiguity, and the usefulness and value of knowledge (Park and Moon 2004).

Others may also find information on a wide range of topics useful, such as domain-specific expertise, project experience, technical information, and market information. While one or more members of an online community may share such information, the decision is entirely theirs (Li 2011). Information controlled by one or a few individuals, but that is valuable to other members of the community, is referred to as discretionary information. There are numerous ways to share such confidential information. Computer technology and the Internet have especially simplified and streamlined the process of storing and retrieving such data (Li 2011). The most common method of information exchange today is the sharing of arbitrary information over computer networks (Li 2011).

Within an organization, widespread information contributions remain the exception rather than the rule. On the contrary, information hoarding and suspicion of information provided by others is a natural human tendency (Davenport and Prusak 1998). Many, if not most, businesses actively limit information contributions owing to concerns about confidentiality, industrial espionage, and diverting or overloading employees with work-related attention (Constant et al. 1994). The organizational incentive structures (such as pay-for-performance schemes) of a firm may, in fact, discourage information contribution if employees believe that providing information will jeopardize their personal efforts to distinguish themselves from their colleagues (Huber 2001). Such a work environment that is not conducive to information sharing is difficult to change once it has been established (Ruggles 1998).

The influencing factors of knowledge management can be summarized and sorted based on a broad overview of the qualitative and quantitative research; they can generally be analyzed from the perspective of several dimensions, including individual, organizational, and technical. The review of the literature thereof showed that more than half of the studies listed human and technological factors as key influencing factors. In Heisig's (2009) study, in particular, over 40 percent of respondents named "organizational factors" as another key influencer.

2.4.1 Individual Factors

Employee motivation and knowledge-sharing behavior are fixtures of the discussion on self-determination theory (Deci and Ryan 2000). Deci and Ryan (2000), in particular, distinguish between two motivation types based on different goals and reasons for action: *intrinsic motivation* and *extrinsic motivation.*

Intrinsic motivation is driven by interest in the task itself, enjoyment, or a willingness to help others; it exists within the individual rather than relying on any external pressure or other reward. People who are intrinsically motivated are more likely to engage in tasks and work to improve their skills, which, in turn, can improve organizational productivity (Deci and Ryan 2000). Extrinsic motivation is the manifestation of an activity that results in a desired outcome. It is focused on an orientation toward goals such as monetary rewards and personal career advancement (Deci and Ryan 2000).

Extrinsic motivation is typically based on perceptions of the costs (efforts) and benefits (rewards) of knowledge and information sharing. When people perceive benefits that outweigh or equal costs, they share their knowledge and information. Many organizations exploit this tendency by implementing reward systems that encourage employees to share their knowledge and information. Both intrinsic and extrinsic motivations are seen as drivers or determinants of knowledge-sharing behaviors in the literature on knowledge management (Wang and Hou 2015).

Trust is also an important influential factor in knowledge sharing. It is the belief that another party will behave appropriately and not take advantage of the situation (Gefen et al. 2003; Hsu et al. 2007), and it exists at both the individual (as interpersonal trust) and organizational or social levels (Hau et al. 2013; Chow and Chan 2008). Employee interaction is especially influenced by social trust, as well as how much employees want to learn from each other and share their knowledge (Chow and Chan 2008).

2.4.2 Organizational Factors

Organizational or corporate culture constitutes the values, beliefs, and systems that promote or inhibit knowledge creation and information sharing within a company (Newell et al. 2009; Janz and Prasarnphanich 2003; Alavi and Leidner 2001; Michailova and Minbaeva 2012). The motivation of an employee to contribute knowledge and information may also be influenced by friendly relations among employees and organizational culture (Hung et al. 2011)—an extremely powerful factor that can influence individuals' day-to-day work practices (Lauring, 2009).

More relevant to this research, organizational culture is also linked to national culture. Noh (2021) argues that shared culture exists in the values, beliefs, and attitudes of groups; and that based on people's values and cultural differences, this affects whether social networking service (SNS) users are familiar with disseminating information. For example, earlier research by Bock et al. (2005) and Davenport and Prusak (1998) argues that shared cultures maintain concepts that tend to effectively guide the use of information management tools and are beneficial for encouraging information-sharing behavior. As cultural sharing stimulates the free flow of information, people are willing to share a large amount of useful information with other users (Hult et al. 2003; Raban and Rafaeli 2007).

In Noh's (2021) study, community openness within an information-sharing culture is seen as an individual tendency, usually associated with more positive information-sharing beliefs. Noh thus explores the diversity of shared cultures; measures and analyzes projects from the perspective of fairness, openness, and identity; and finds that it affects the extent to which SNS users disseminate information in shared cultural environments.

I also briefly review the effect of organizational citizen behavior (OCB) on information sharing in organizational influencing factors. Social exchange theory (Blau 1964) states that knowledge and information sharing is a way of social interaction. It further attributes information sharing to behavioral factors such as job security, status, the balance of power, and maintenance of future relationships (Bock et al. 2005; Cabrera and Cabrera 2005; Jarvenpaa and Staples 2001; Muthusamy et al. 2007). Information sharing is a form of OCB, which is a voluntary act that contributes to an organization's competitive advantage. OCB is known to significantly affect information-sharing behavior (Al-Zu'bi 2011; Ramasamy and Thamaraiselvan 2011; Teh and Yong, 2011; Islam et al. 2012; Teh and Sun 2012; Husain and Husain 2016). This means that the more employees there are that exhibit OCB, the higher their information-sharing behavior.

2.4.3 Technological Factors

Technology is a core factor and an important driver of managing knowledge and knowledge sharing in an organization. Technology use, functionality, and usability (Kirchner et al. 2009); contribution "requires too much time and effort" (Vuori and Okkonen 2012); platform structure (Matschke et al. 2014); "interface design and user needs" (Hung et al. 2011); and other factors are considered to be important factors in employee knowledge and information contribution.

According to recent research, corporate social media is a facilitator of new ways of working and new forms of knowledge sharing and interaction (Razmerita et al. 2016). I hypothesize that, depending on the internal context of the organization, technology can not only improve information self-efficacy, connectivity effectiveness, and levels of cooperation among employees, but it can also reduce user motivation (e.g., when contribution costs are high) (Cabrera and Cabrera 2002).

I analyze and summarize the influencing factors of information contribution in several dimensions based on the literature review. Although these are not the only influencing factors, I focus on the factors of personal motivation dimension and the motivation of individuals to contribute information in the organization. In Table 1-1, I classify the literature on this topic.

Table 1-1. Literature Review on Influencing Factors of Information Contribution

Influencing Factors	Classification	Literature Review	Source
Individual Factors	Intrinsic Motivation	Intrinsic motivation is driven by interest in the task itself, enjoyment, or a willingness to help others, and that exists within the individual rather than relying on any external pressure or other reward. People who are intrinsically motivated are more likely to engage in tasks and work to improve their skills, which, in turn, can improve organizational productivity (Deci and Ryan 2000).	Deci and Ryan (2000)
	Extrinsic Motivation	Extrinsic motivation is the manifestation of an activity that results in a desired outcome. It focuses on goal-oriented motivations such as monetary rewards and personal career advancement (Deci and Ryan 2000).	Deci and Ryan (2000); Wang and Hou (2015)
	Interpersonal Trust	Trust influences knowledge sharing. It can be discussed at the individual level, such as interpersonal trust and organization, or at various social levels, such as class (Hau et al. 2013; Chow and Chan 2008).	Hau et al. (2013); Chow and Chan (2008)

Table 1-2. Literature Review on Influencing Factors of Information Contribution

Influencing Factors	Classification	Literature Review	Source
Organizational Factors	Organizational Trust	Trust is the belief that the other party will behave appropriately and will not take advantage of the situation (Gefen et al. 2003; Hsu et al. 2007). Employee interactions are influenced by social and organizational trust, that is, how much they want to learn from each other and share their knowledge (Chow and Chan 2008).	Gefen et al. (2003); Hsu et al. (2007); Chow and Chan (2008)
	Organizational Culture	Organizational or corporate culture can be defined as the values, beliefs, and systems that promote or inhibit knowledge creation and information sharing within a company (Newell et al. 2009; Janz and Prasarnphanich 2003; Alavi and Leidner 2001; Michailova and Minbaeva 2012). Employee motivation to contribute knowledge and information may also be influenced by organizational culture and friendly relations among employees (Hung et al. 2011).	Newell et al. (2009)
	National Cultural	Organizational culture is linked to national culture. According to Lauring (2009), organizational culture is extremely powerful and can influence an individual's day-to-day work practices.	Lauring (2009)

Table 1-3. Literature Review on Influencing Factors of Information Contribution

Influencing Factors	Classification	Literature Review	Source
Organizational Factors	Sharing Cultural	Noh (2021) argues that shared culture exists in the values, beliefs, and attitudes of groups. Based on people's values and cultural differences, this affects whether SNS users are familiar with disseminating information. For example, shared cultures maintain concepts that tend to effectively guide the use of information management tools and are beneficial for encouraging information shared behavior (Bock et al. 2005; Davenport and Prusak 1998; Davenport et al. 1998). As cultural sharing stimulates the free flow of information, people are willing to share a large amount of useful information with other users (Hult et al. 2003; Raban and Rafaeli 2007). In the Noh (2021) study, community openness within an information-sharing culture is seen as an individual tendency, usually associated with more positive information-sharing beliefs. Noh (2021) explores the diversity of shared cultures; measures and analyzes projects from the perspective of fairness, openness, and identity; and finds that it affects the extent to which SNS users disseminate information in shared cultural environments.	Davenport and Prusak (1998); Hult et al. (2003); Bock et al. (2005); Raban and Rafaeli (2007); Noh (2021)

	Organizational Citizen Behavior	Information sharing is a form of OCB—a voluntary act that contributes to an organization's competitive advantage. OCB has a significant effect on information-sharing behavior (Al-Zu'bi 2011; Ramasamy and Thamaraiselvan 2011; Teh and Yong 2011; Islam et al. 2012; Teh and Sun 2012; Husain and Husain 2016). This means that the more employees exhibit OCB, the higher their information-sharing behavior.	Husain and Husain (2016); Teh and Sun (2012)
Technological Factors	Technical Usefulness Technical Ease of Use Technology Application	Technology as a core factor is an important driver for managing knowledge and knowledge sharing in an organization. Technology use and functionality, usability (Kirchner et al. 2008), that contribution "requires too much time and effort" (Vuori and Okkonen 2012), platform structure (Matschke et al. 2014), and "interface design and user needs" (Hung et al. 2011) are considered important factors of employee knowledge and information contribution. According to recent research, corporate social media is a facilitator of new ways of working and new forms of knowledge sharing and interaction (Razmerita et al. 2016). This study hypothesizes that, depending on the internal context of the organization, technology can not only improve information self-efficacy, connectivity effectiveness, and levels of cooperation among employees, but it can also reduce user motivation (e.g., when contribution costs are high) (Cabrera 2002).	Razmerita et al. (2016); Cabrera (2002)

The literature review confirms that organizational influencing factors (organizational trust, organizational culture, national culture, shared culture, organizational citizen behavior, etc.) affect employees' information contribution (Hung et al. 2011; Bock et al. 2005; Noh 2021; Husain and Husain 2016). However, these factors may be limited by external changes, including external environmental factors, which ultimately affect information contribution. Technical factors can affect the efficiency of communication and collaboration among employees contributing information, and also reduce user motivation (e.g., when contribution costs are high) (Cabrera and Cabrera 2002).

This study focuses on individual influencing factors, including intrinsic and extrinsic motivation. I thus define intrinsic motivation as that driven by interest in the task itself, enjoyment, or a willingness to help others; its source is internal, that is, within the individual, than based in external pressures or rewards. People who are intrinsically motivated are more likely to engage in tasks and strive to improve their skills, which can ultimately increase organizational productivity (Deci and Ryan 2000). Alternatively, extrinsic motivation is focused on goal-oriented motivation, such as monetary rewards and personal career development (Deci and Ryan 2000). Extrinsic motivation is usually based on perceptions of the costs (efforts) and benefits (rewards) of knowledge and information sharing. When people believe the benefits are greater than or equal to the costs, they share their knowledge and information.

I conduct an in-depth investigation of an individual factor (motivation), and then combine the expectancy theory and the characteristics of the Chinese corporate relationship culture to develop the variable of a personal factor (motivation) to apply it to an information contribution model.

2.5 Theoretical Development

In the theoretical review of the influencing factors of information contribution, I focus on two main factors of performance and relationship expectations based on expectancy theory, Chinese relationship culture, work engagement, and information contribution, with the mediating effect of work engagement on information contribution intention.

I use expectancy theory as the general framework to study the direct effect of performance and relationship expectations on information-contributing behavior. Expectancy theory will help us understand the intrinsic manifestation of motivation, the study's main focus. Recall that intrinsic motivation is an interest in the task itself and not rooted in any external pressure or reward. Intrinsically motivated people, as noted earlier, increase organizational productivity (Deci and Ryan 2000). Relatedly, work engagement positively affects employees' willingness to share knowledge (Song et al. 2014; Chen et al. 2011; Tang et al. 2015). Engaged employees are mentally, emotionally, and physically connected and integrated, and focused on their roles. According to Kahn (1990), such employees are not only open to themselves and others, but also to work and others because they are fully committed to their work (Kahn 1990). Combined with the cultural characteristics of China's SMEs, I go into the greater details of relationship expectations.

The literature on people's motivation to contribute to a pool of information and the factors that lead to solutions to communication dilemmas provides a foundation for developing the hypotheses about information-contributing behaviors (Li 2011).

2.5.1 Expectancy Theory

This section discusses and explains expectancy theory from the perspective of organizational members' expectations of organizational performance and relationships. In terms of motivational expectancy theory, let us look at Vroom's (1964) theoretical study, which states that personal assessment options are chosen based on which options are thought to lead to the most desirable personal outcomes. Expectancy theory is a cognitive theory of motivation that focuses on human subjective rational behavior. It comprises three core concepts—expectations, tools, and valence—which when combined produce motivational forces. Expectancy theory was initially developed to explain motivation, specifically a voluntary choice made by individuals when alternatives are available. When applied to a job role, it focuses on three areas: decision making, satisfaction, and performance levels.

According to expectancy theory, people actively monitor the outcomes of their actions and assess the likelihood of those actions resulting in specific positive outcomes. Accordingly, the desire for reward determines an individual's motivation to perform certain actions. The willingness to put in the effort to achieve a specific outcome is thus determined by several factors, including (a) the value that will be assessed on the return, (b) the likelihood that those outcomes will yield a return, and (c) the likelihood of achieving the ultimate goal (Isaac et al. 2001; Li 2011). In the past, researchers have used expectancy theory to investigate the factors that lead to system acceptance and intention to use as well (Ajzen and Fishbein 1980; DeSanctis 1983; Snead and Harrell 1994; Li 2011).

Employee motivation and knowledge-sharing behaviors are often discussed in self-determination theory (Deci and Ryan 2000). According to Passer and Smith (2004), the concept of "motivation" refers to the processes that influence the direction, persistence, and vitality of goal-directed behavior. Likewise, Coetsee (2003) states that the term "motivation" refers to the interaction between forces within an individual and his/her environment. Kreitner and Kinicki (2007) argue that, in the current context, motivation represents the mental processes that lead to arousal, direction, and persistence of voluntary behavior. Likewise, Werner (2002) describes motivation as intentional (one chooses to act) and directional (indicating the presence of a drive aimed at achieving a particular goal). Applied in a work context, motivation is the willingness of individuals and teams to put in a high level of effort to achieve organizational goals, conditioned on the ability to strive to meet individual and team needs (Coetsee 2003). As noted earlier, Deci and Ryan distinguished motivation in extrinsic and intrinsic in terms of one's goals, and the latter is the subject of my focus. We can understand motivation as a process that affects behaviors that improve organizational performance and personal relationships. It is the interaction between the internal strength of an individual and his/her organizational environment—a psychological process that leads to the persistence of information-contributing behavior.

Expectancy theory holds that people choose between alternative behavioral plans based on their perceptions (expectations) of how well a given behavior will lead to a desired outcome. Transactions such as payment for services rendered typically occur in organizational employment relationships between the employer (provider of incentives and recognition) and the employee (provider of service) (Dawson 2000). *Ceteris paribus*, Robinson (1992) shows a link between transactional leadership and stimulus-response theory because incentives (in the form of rewards, salaries, rewards, etc.) are used to ensure expectations are met. Responses and organizational outcomes are thus reproduced and repeated.

However, in most transactional relationships, managerial power and authority are absolute and unassailable, to the point where employees become production system automatons. Those deemed productive receive rewards, whereas those deemed unproductive and competitive are pushed out of the system (Mathibe 2008).

Expectations, effort, productivity, and rewards all have a delicate relationship. DeSimon et al. (2002) state that, if a person believes that there is a reasonable chance that his/her efforts will help achieve organizational goals, and that this achievement will be a tool, he/she will exert more effort. It will be used by the individual to achieve his/her personal objectives. If this is the case, organizational goals will take precedence over personal goals, which may explain why incentives and rewards are used to recognize employee efforts.

The literature establishes that when an employer and an employee enter into an employment relationship, both parties have expectations. Kotter (1976) explains the expectations of employers and employees, making two groups of comparisons and offering two perspectives. The first set of expectations represents what the individual expects from the organization and what the organization expects to give to the individual, while the second set of expectations represents what the individual expects to bring to the organization. These two expectations represent a relationship of compromise intended to produce a win–win situation for both the employee and the organization. Such inclusion expectations are the "dynamics of organization–individual interactions" (Mathibe 2008).

The psychological contract, according to Kreitner and Kinicki (2007), is the perception of the terms and associated conditions by which an individual makes a reciprocal exchange with another party. Schein (1980) summarizes the significance of expectations succinctly and clearly:

... one of my central assumptions is that whether a person develops dedication, loyalty, and enthusiasm for an organization and its goals is largely determined by two factors: These include: (1) the degree to which his own expectations of what the organization will provide him with what he owes organization match with what the organizations are of what it will give and get; (2) assuming there is agreement on expectations what actually is to be exchanged...

It may be argued that both employers and employees must convey their expectations.

Expected relationship refers to a personal desire that arises for relationship formation when an individual is placed in a situation where he/she can form a new relationship with the members of the community to which he/she belongs (Lee et al. 2020). Nadri et al. (2004) and Lee et al. (2020) also agree that communication in a virtual space helps maintain social networks by upholding existing relationships and reestablishing old relationships with weak influence. The authors explain that individuals form a habit of creating and maintaining intimate, appropriate relationships. This strengthens the intimacy of existing relationships, while a new human network is also formed that allows one to connect to the virtual space at any free time or communicate with someone constantly through information sharing (Lee et al. 2020).

Mellor et al. (2001) explains that factors such as whether to share experiences with the other party and the existence of dialogue that can give the other party a sense of stability and promote exchange are important resources for relationship formation. On the formation of online relationships, studies emphasize real person-to-person contact, while also insisting on exchanges with "real people" (Mellor et al. 2001; Lee et al. 2020).

Relationship of expectations features in studies on online social interactions and on the determinants of the level of participation of Internet users. Such a relationship has a positive effect on the immersion of online communities and the effectiveness of the Internet (Emde et al. 2020; Lee et al. 2020). It also significantly affects perceived usefulness and perceived ease of use in the formation of immersive online communities in technology acceptance models (Nadri et al. 2004; Lee et al. 2020).

2.5.2 China's Relationship Culture

It is widely assumed that Chinese societies emphasize on *guanxi* exchanges. Chinese enterprises similarly conduct economic transactions and maintain social exchanges based on this philosophy. In this article, *guanxi* is understood to mean "relationship"; that is, a special social relationship based on mutual benefit, mutual responsibility for resource acquisition, and ongoing cooperation, or *reciprocity*. Relationships are the fundamental link that allow today's Chinese enterprises and Chinese people to maintain economic and social activities.

Personal relationships are highly valued in Chinese society as the foundation of economic and social organization (Hwang 1987). Although it is among individuals, the relationship is built on reciprocal exchanges between members of the "inner circle" (Hwang 1987; Fei 1992). This is a unique way of social composition in today's China, where "who you know" is more important than "what you know" (Yeung and Tung 1996).

In China, people believe that, in daily life and business dealings, *guanxi* can improve the competitiveness of enterprises, help easily obtain scarce resources when necessary, and make long-term survival and development possible (Tsang 1998; Luo 1997; Yeung and Tung 1996).

From a theoretical point of view, the motivation of the relationship, as constructed by Chinese enterprises and the Chinese, can be explained in three ways. First, from a sociological point of view, relationship emphasizes feelings and their maintenance. Emotional retention is common among close friends and family members, where social exchange mainly follows the law of needs; that is, resource allocation is not based on members' contributions to the organization, but rather on their individual needs. It is usually difficult for resource allocators to meet the requirements of all members. By convention, beneficiary members will return the benefits and resources they have received in the past. Such a relationship has the characteristics of "face," and "face" is a manifestation of Chinese people's lack of affection. Second, from an economic point of view, the focus is on transaction fees. Relationship cannot only reduce transaction costs, but also improve transaction efficiency. Third, from the legal standpoint, the family-centered relationship network has been strengthened in the absence of a complete legal system. In the context of a well-established legal system, Chinese companies and Chinese people try to find personal power within the trust-based relationship network for protection (Davies et al. 1995).

Noh and Kang (2021) state that the motivation for obtaining personal information is to maintain interpersonal relationships or friendships. Their analysis shows that Chinese respondents mostly emphasized friendship, which highlights the characteristics of Chinese relationship culture.

Personal information-sharing activities are motivated by a desire to improve interpersonal communication (Noh and Kang 2021). Noh et al. (2022) also point to the belief that these mutual relationships can be improved through knowledge sharing; and in the interest of fairness and reciprocity, employees who operate on desire may have a positive attitude toward information sharing.

I consider the relationship motivation and expectancy theory to expound on the relationship between members of China's SMEs and the relationship between members and the organization. This study especially focuses on expectation reciprocity and relationship expectation.

2.5.3 Relationship Networks and Knowledge Sharing within Enterprises

Guanxi is a concept that describes the relationship between individuals and business networks in China (Luo et al. 2012). Hitt et al.'s (2002) view is that the mutually beneficial relationship of obligation between Chinese ties and Korean personal ties is established among people who share visible and meaningful experiences.

Ordonez de Pablos (2005) states that the emotional relationship among individuals implies the development of close relationships with others. Ultimately, he notes, there is an emotional connection between two different organizations. In other words, *guanxi* is a very important strategic and organizational factor that constitutes an intimate and powerful network in business relationships between individuals and companies in China (Gao et al. 2014).

Note that knowledge sharing is the exchange of knowledge possessed by members of an enterprise organization with other enterprise organizations through networks that are transformed into assets and resources (Lai et al. 2010). In this context, researchers have studied knowledge sharing among firms in the form of knowledge transfer. Easterby-Smith et al. (2008) propose that knowledge transfer is bidirectional, as the relationship between two parties in the network (such as strategic alliances and consumers/suppliers) changes. Lu et al. (2013) argue that knowledge transfer is a process in which a company is influenced by other companies through a network.

Lu et al. (2006) believe that, knowledge dissemination and

technology transfer among companies can be promoted through informal communication and exchanges such as establishing social networks. Knowledge can be created and utilized across networks for commercial purposes (Moller et al. 2004). Vithessonthi (2008), however, caution that knowledge learning among firms is possible not only through contracts among managers, but also by exchanging important knowledge.

Knowledge sharing among partner companies and among bilateral companies is inseparable from relationship formation; similarly, information contribution among corporate employees is inseparable from relationships—at least in the "relationship-oriented society" of China (Gao et al. 2014). This is why *guanxi* has such an importance place in Chinese business networks; it informs all business practices, and is a singular cultural factor that connects networks of mutually beneficial relationships as well as networks of mutually beneficial relationships among employees.

This way, I consider *guanxi* to be a business relationship network among alliance partners, and thus a factor of knowledge sharing among enterprises and information contribution among employees.

2.5.4 Work Engagement and Information Contribution

The intention of employees to share knowledge depends on their work engagement (Song et al. 2014; Chen et al. 2011; Tang et al. 2015). Yet, the probable link between work engagement and knowledge sharing is underappreciated (Chen et al. 2011).

I examine a number of studies wherein engagement is defined as, on the one hand, promoting connections with work and others, and on the other hand, performing task behaviors while simultaneously using and expressing one's "preferred self" (Kahn 1990). As noted before, engaged employees are focused, self-confident, open to others, and committed to their work (Kahn 1990).

The increased attention toward work and employee engagement has led to the emergence of varied conceptualizations and definitions thereof. According to Schaufeli et al. (2002), the most widely used and recognized definition of work engagement is "a positive, gratifying, job-related state of mind marked by energy, devotion, and immersion." Individuals who are passionate about their work often have more energy and mental resilience; they put in a lot of effort (vigor) in the activities that they do. Such engaged personnel are invested in their work, and experience a sense of purpose, excitement, inspiration, pride, and challenge.

According to Shuck and Wollard (2010), comparable definitions of work engagement exist in the literature, such as personal engagement, behavior engagement, and trait engagement, and each provides a unique perspective and context. For the purposes of this study, the term "work engagement" is chosen and defined in accordance with the previously described terms. Work engagement, when compared with other related concepts, encompasses a wide range of aspects of the employee engagement experience (e.g., cognitive, emotional, and physical). It is the intentional involvement with or attachment to tasks, objectives, or organizational activities at the cognitive, emotional, and physical level by, for example, having a positive self-perception of one's effectiveness, feeling positive emotions about executing tasks, and voluntarily utilizing one's energy and effort to achieve those tasks (Castaneda and Durán 2018; Kuok and Taormina 2017).

Work engagement is a key factor in determining organizational performance and success. It has already shown to influence organizational outcomes such as job satisfaction, organizational commitment, and organizational citizenship behavior (Bailey et al. 2017; Andrew and Sofian 2012; Saks 2006). We know that employee work engagement improves the intention to share knowledge (Song et al. 2014; Chen et al. 2011; Tang et al. 2015). Such employees are more likely to share ideas and expertise (Chen et al. 2011), and the resulting job satisfaction has a profound influence on increased innovative behaviors at work (Agarwal 2014; Agarwal et al. 2012; De Spiegelaere et al. 2016).

On the relationship between information sharing and innovative work behavior (Radaelli et al. 2014; Kim and Park 2015; Yu, et al. 2013), we know that employees are more likely to elaborate, integrate, and translate information when they share their expertise (Radaelli et al. 2014) than when they simply pass it along to receivers. This activity encourages employees to engage in creative work behaviors such as looking for opportunities for change and implementing new ideas into existing organizational procedures. Taken together, increased employee work engagement may have a positive effect on knowledge-sharing and creative behavior.

Work engagement encompasses experiences at the cognitive, emotional, and physical level; it is the intentional involvement with or attachment to tasks, objectives, or organizational activities (Castaneda and Durán 2018; Kuok and Taormina 2017). The strong correlation between work engagement and information sharing in organizations also provides a strong basis for the selection of work engagement as a construct.

Reviewing this literature allows in-depth research and development of expectancy theory within the context of performance expectation motivation and relational expectation motivation. I investigate the relationship expectation by considering guanxi among Chinese SMEs. In terms of variable definitions, as per the unified theory of acceptance and use of technology model, performance expectation is defined as the extent to which a person believes that using the system can help improve the performance of a task, whereas social influence is the perception that important people around them believe they should use the new system (Venkatesh et al. 2003; Venkatesh e al. 2012). In this study, performance expectation is defined as the extent to which organizational and individual performance can be improved through information contribution. Here, relationship expectation is considered a social influencing factor, defined as the extent to which a relationship with members of an organization could be improved and maintained through information contribution. Finally, intention and behavioral factors are also part of the composition of this study. My model draws from the theory of reasoned action (TRA). I further discuss intention as a good predictor of behavior (Ajzen 1991; Fishbein and Ajzen 1975), where intention is defined as self-instruction for carrying out a particular action to achieve a particular result (Triandis 1979), and, in turn, a person's actions are the visible manifestation of their actions (Triandis 1979; Millikan and Woodfield 1993). Given the theoretical basis of information-sharing intention and knowledge-sharing behaviors, I add information-contribution intention and information-contribution behavior into my model.

Chapter 3

III. Research Model and Hypothesis Development

3.1 Research Model

Based on expectancy theory, this research model introduces performance and relationship expectation, and work engagement through the correlation between work engagement and information contribution. I make appropriate modifications and improvements to the TRA model.

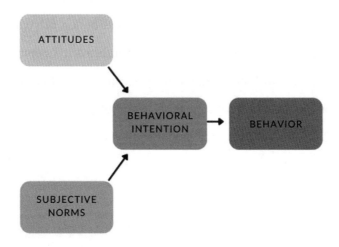

TRA was developed by Fishbein and Ajzen in 1975. It is mainly used to analyze how attitudes consciously affect individual behavior, and lends insight into how attitudes are formed based on cognitive information. TRA focuses on the intention to engage in certain behavior. It is especially popular among scholars developing psychosocial models that explain human behavior, and is actually an expansion of expectancy theory, which includes environmental factors in addition to the differences among individuals. Within this context, individual motivation is a function of attitudes that stem from one's hopes to realize one's potential to achieve desired outcomes through certain behaviors.

However, my research model deviates from the conventional TRA model in three ways: 1) performance and relationship expectations directly affect the information contribution intention and work engagement; 2) information contribution intention and work engagement directly affect information contribution behavior; and 3) the degree of the mediating effect of information contribution intention and work engagement on performance and relationship expectations affects the information contribution behavior. Figures 1 and 2 illustrate the research model and hypotheses, respectively.

Figure 1. Researcher Development Model

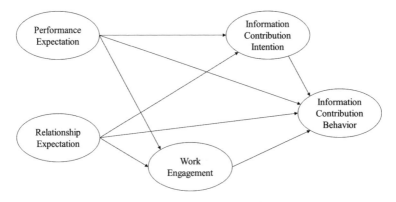

Figure 2. Hypothesis Relationship Model

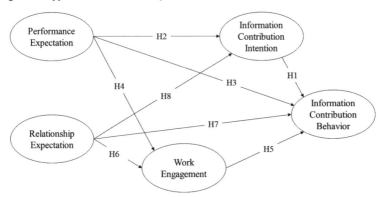

H9 = Performance Expectation → Information Contribution Intention → Information Contribution Behavior; H10 = Relationship Expectation → Information Contribution Intention → Information Contribution Behavior; H11 = Performance Expectation → Work Engagement → Information Contribution Behavior; H12 = Relationship Expectation → Work Engagement → Information Contribution Behavior

3.2 Hypothesis Development

Through a detailed review of the literature, I formulate the hypotheses based on the model and variables shown in Figure 2. The eight hypotheses are listed in Table 2.

Table 2. Hypothesis Development

Items	Hypothesis
Hypothesis 1	Information contribution intention has a positive effect on information contribution behavior.
Hypothesis 2	Performance expectation has a positive effect on information contribution intention.
Hypothesis 3	Performance expectation has a positive effect on information contribution behavior.
Hypothesis 4	Performance expectation has a positive effect on work engagement.
Hypothesis 5	Work engagement has a positive effect on information contribution behavior.
Hypothesis 6	Relationship expectation has a positive effect on work engagement.
Hypothesis 7	Relationship expectation has a positive effect on information contribution intention.
Hypothesis 8	Relationship expectation has a positive effect on information contribution behavior.
Hypothesis 9	Performance expectation indirectly affects information contribution behavior through information contribution intention.
Hypothesis 10	Relationship expectation indirectly affects information contribution behavior through information contribution intention.

| Hypothesis 11 | Performance expectation indirectly affects information contribution behavior through work engagement. |
| Hypothesis 12 | Relationship expectation indirectly affects information contribution behavior through work engagement. |

The close relationship between intention and behavior is based in theory and empirical evidence (Armitage and Conner 2001). The literature on behavioral intentions defines knowledge-sharing behavior as the dissemination of knowledge and information acquired by one member to other members within a virtual community (Lin et al. 2009; Ryu et al. 2003), while creative commons intention is the degree to which a member believes a person will engage in knowledge-sharing behaviors (Bock et al. 2005).

Behavioral intention is a strong predictor of actual behavior according to the theory of planned behavior (Ajzen 1991); there exists substantial empirical evidence supporting this relationship (see Kim et al. 2008; Pavlou and Fygenson 2006; Venkatesh and Davis 2000). I thus anticipate that the willingness to contribute information will positively influence behavior to this effect.

Intention is also a good predictor of behavior (Ajzen 1991; Fishbein and Ajzen 1975); it is defined as performing a specific action or self-indication of actions to achieve a specific outcome (Triandis 1979). A person's actions are visible manifestations of their actions (Triandis 1979; Millikan and Woodfield 1993).

Indeed, Castaneda and Durán (2016) confirm a positive relationship between knowledge-sharing intentions and knowledge-sharing behaviors in public organizations. I thus hypothesize:

Hypothesis 1: Information contribution intention has a positive effect on information contribution behavior.

Expectancy theory explains how a decision-making action is motivated by the desire for a reward (Vroom 1964; Li 2011). This theory assumes that people actively monitor the outcomes of their actions and assess the likelihood that those actions will result in specific positive outcomes, such a reward. An individual's desire to receive this reward determines the motivation for certain behaviors. Thus, the willingness to exert effort to achieve a result can be determined by several factors, including (a) the value that can potentially be received as a reward; (b) the likelihood that a performance will generate returns; and (c) the achievement of performance outcomes the possibility of the target (Isaac et al. 2001; Li 2011). Expectancy theory has also been used to investigate the factors that lead to system acceptance and intention to use (Ajzen and Fishbein 1980; DeSanctis 1983; Snead and Harrell 1994; Li 2011).

According to social exchange theory, outcome expectations refer to the expected outcome of one's behavior (Bandura 1997; Compeau and Higgins 1995), and an individual's conduct may result in a beneficial outcome because people act in their own best interests (Bock and Kim 2002). Such positive expectancies can be viewed as incentives within each form, and human behavior is influenced by these various types of influences (Bandura 1997). Social cognitive theory lends further credence to this belief, as it states that individuals are more likely to engage in behaviors that they expect to lead to positive outcomes. In this study, individual outcome expectation refers to the information contributor's judgment that his/her information-contribution behavior will help achieve performance and organizational outcomes, whereas organization-related outcome expectation refers to the information contributor's judgment that his/her information contribution will help achieve performance and organizational outcomes (Chiu et al. 2006).

According to the efficiency-oriented perspective, employees share knowledge that will allow them to produce the outputs that will help them achieve their goals more efficiently (Abrahamson 1991). For employees, information-sharing behavior and innovation improves their performance at and efficiency in achieving professional outcomes.

Positive performance outcomes include increased productivity and work quality, a lower error rate, a greater ability to meet goals and objectives, and overall improvements in job performance (Yuan and Woodman 2010). Employees may share information to improve the efficiency of their work roles and units. This increased job performance allows them to be more competitive and successful.

I interpret individual outcome expectations based on the hypotheses developed in established literature. That is, the effects of both outcome and performance expectations are the same. I thus hypothesize:

> *Hypothesis 2: Performance expectation has a positive effect on information contribution intention.*
>
> *Hypothesis 3: Performance expectation has a positive effect on information contribution behavior.*
>
> *Hypothesis 9: Performance expectation indirectly affects information contribution behavior through information contribution intention.*

Employees with high intrinsic motivation spend more time on organizational activities, have pleasanter moods, and experience less anxiety in the workplace (Deci and Ryan 1980). They are more engaged with their work because they are driven. If an employee's work engagement leads to performance-related rewards, he/she is likely to be more involved with his/her work.

As per the concept of social exchange, relationships are a major determinant of two individuals' attitudes and motivations when they are influenced by their social and organizational environment, particularly when exchanging unspecified cooperative outputs such as knowledge. Unlike economic transactions, social exchange results in friendship and/or authority over others, as well as broad, uncertain commitments (Organ and Konovsky 1989). The main concern is the relationship itself, rather than any direct extrinsic benefit (Blau 1967). Employees who believe that work engagement can improve their reciprocal relationships (i.e., social exchange) with others and are motivated by a desire for fairness and reciprocity are more likely to have positive attitudes and motivations toward work engagement (Huber 2001). I surmise that increasing performance expectation and such relationship expectations will increase work engagement. I thus hypothesize:

Hypothesis 4: Performance expectation has a positive effect on work engagement.

Hypothesis 6: Relationship expectation has a positive effect on work engagement.

Hypothesis 11: Performance expectation indirectly affects information contribution behavior through work engagement.

Hypothesis 12: Relationship expectation indirectly affects information contribution behavior through work engagement.

There is an established role of work engagement as a mediator in the relationship between antecedents and outcomes in organizational settings (Kim et al. 2012). The literature (Wang and Noe 2010; Song et al. 2014, Agarwal 2014; Radaelli et al. 2014; Schepers and Van den Berg 2007) indicates that, if organizations are serious about decision-making fairness, they will facilitate and support employee work engagement, which, in turn, enhances employees' readiness to share their job-related knowledge with other organizational members and/or actively promote new ideas for their company. This process may then lead to application of ideas with the help of peers and/or managers, namely, innovative behavior.

Empirical evidence supports the influence of job engagement on positive organizational outcomes such as job satisfaction, organizational commitment, and organizational citizenship behavior, as well as negative outcomes such as intention to resign (Bailey 2017; Andrew and Sofian 2012; Saks 2006). Yet, there is limited research on work engagement and knowledge sharing (Chen et al. 2011).

Our literature review already confirms the positive relationship between information sharing and innovative and creative work behavior (Radaelli 2014; Kim and Park 2015; Yu et al. 2013) among driven employees. As increased employee work engagement may have a positive effect on knowledge sharing and creative behavior, I thus hypothesize:

Hypothesis 5: Work engagement has a positive effect on information contribution behavior.

Lastly, expected relationship refers to a personal desire that arises for relationship formation when an individual is placed in a situation where he/she can form a new relationship with the members of the community to which he/she belongs (Lee et al. 2020). In a virtual space that is not bound by time and or geographical constraints, communication serves to maintain existing relationships, reestablish old relationships with weak influence, and form new human networks through constant information sharing (Nadri et al. 2004; Lee et al. 2020). However, we cannot discount person-to-person contact in exchanges with real people (Barnes 2001; Lee et al. 2020). Barnes (2001) further explains that relationships are formed by deciding whether to share experiences and through dialogue that promotes a relation's stability and exchange. Indeed, such a relationship of expectations makes online communities more immersive (Lee et al. 2020), and it has a significant effect on the perceived usefulness and perceived ease of use of immersive online communities in the technology acceptance model (Nadri et al.

2004; Lee et al. 2020).

I draw on the literature discussed above to understand the formation of employee relationships within the organization. Relationship formation is the premise of communication among employees. Only strong relationships can create a successful relationship network, allowing employees to communicate continuously through information sharing and information contribution. I argue that information contribution will be higher as a result of increased relationship expectations. I thus hypothesize:

Hypothesis 7: Relationship expectation has a positive effect on information contribution intention.

Hypothesis 8: Relationship expectation has a positive effect on information contribution behavior.

Hypothesis 10: Relationship expectation indirectly affects information contribution behavior through information contribution intention.

Chapter 4

IV. Research Methodology

4.1 Survey Introduction

The study reveals the information contribution behavior between the sender and the receiver within an organization. Managers offer quantitative and qualitative analysis of the business—both aspects have different influences, advantages, and disadvantages. I especially employ a quantitative research technique for the analysis of data.

Quantitative research constitutes data collection and statistical analysis of predefined constructs. Questions are designed in accordance with the research objectives, and the resulting data are analyzed and evaluated to determine their generalizability. Good selection and analysis of data allows us to create an accurate picture of the study objects through reliable and representative information. In this study, I employ questionnaire surveys and specific variables for analysis.

Data analysis to test the hypotheses is done using the Statistical

Package for the Social Science (SPSS) 23.0 program and AMOS 23.0 program. I use a five-point Likert-type scale to measure the constructs of the questionnaire. First, I analyze the respondents based on common characteristics. Second, to ensure validity and reliability of constructs, I conduct factor and reliability analysis. Third, to test the relationships among all variables, I investigate the interactions among them. Finally, I conduct an assessment of the developed model and thoroughly investigate the structure measurement thereof).

4.2 Operational Definition and Structure Measures

Operational definitions are methods of defining the meaning of variables based on observable, quantifiable, and actionable characteristics, that is, to translate abstract notions into observable and testable items by describing the functions of variables derived from specific behaviors, traits, and indications. An operational definition is essentially a thorough explanation of the operational methods and variables evaluated. The operational definition is very significant in empirical research; it forms the foundation for determining whether the study is worthwhile. Table 3 lists the operational definitions of the variables of this study.

Table 3. Operational Definition

Construct Items	Definitions	Items	Key References
Performance Expectation	Performance expectation is the extent to which organizational and individual performance can be improved through information contribution.	5(5)	Venkatesh et al. (2003), Venkatesh et al. (2012)
Relationship Expectation	Relationship expectation is the extent to which the relationship with the members of the organization could be improved and maintained through information contribution.	5(5)	Venkatesh et al. (2012), Lee et al. (2020), Khanam and Parveen (2019)
Work Engagement	The intentional involvement with or attachment to tasks, objectives, or organizational activities cognitively, emotionally, and physically by having positive thoughts about improving one's effectiveness, feeling positive emotions about executing the tasks, and voluntarily utilizing one's energy and effort to achieve those tasks.	9(9)	Castaneda and Durán (2018), Kuok and Taormina (2017)
Information Contribution Intention	The degree to which one believes that one will engage in an explicit information contribution action.	4(4)	Bock et al. (2005)
Information Contribution Behavior	The degree to which one will engage in an explicit information contribution action.	4(4)	Bock et al. (2005)

Measurement scale items corresponding to the variables are proposed based on the literature review. In some cases, parts of the items are canceled or revised owing to semantic mistakes in translation. The scale items are measured on five-point Likert-type scale, with anchors shifting from "strongly disagree" (1) to "strongly agree" (5). To ensure item reliability, the Cronbach's Alpha coefficient is determined. The scales to survey the constructs are indicated in Table 4 of Appendix F. The processing measures of all of construct are proposed in the following section.

4.2.1 Measurement of Performance Expectation

The constructs are assessed using a five-point Likert scale adapted from the literature. Performance expectation, a utility construct, has consistently been shown to be the best predictor of behavioral intention (Venkatesh et al. 2003; Venkatesh et al. 2012; Sair and Danish 2018). Table 4 shows the performance expectation scale with five items for each construct, as modified from the scale by Venkatesh et al. (2012).

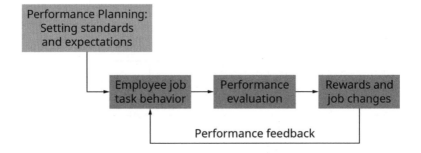

Table 4. Measurement of Performance Expectation

Items	Measures	Key References
Performance Expectation (PE1–PE5)	PE1. I expect that contributing information is useful in firm members' daily work.	Venkatesh et al. (2012)
	PE2. I expect that contributing information will increase firm members' chances of achieving things that are important them.	
	PE3. I expect that contributing information will help firm members get their work done faster.	
	PE4. I expect that contributing information will increase firm productivity.	
	PE5. I expect that contributing information will help achieve firm performance.	

4.2.2 Measurement of Relationship Expectation

Employees who believe that their mutual relationships with others will improve as a result of their information contribution and who are motivated by a desire for justice and reciprocity (Huber 2001) are more likely to have positive attitudes toward information sharing. Relatedly, expected relationship refers to a personal desire that arises for relationship formation when an individual is placed in a situation where he/she can form a new relationship with the members of the community to which he/she belongs (Lee et al. 2020). The main focus is on the relationship itself, rather than any potential external advantage (Blau 1967). In this study, the scale for relationship expectation has three items and is based on the scale developed by Sparrowe and Liden (1997), Khanam and Parveen (2019), and Lee et al. (2020), as shown in Table 5.

Table 5. Measurement of Relationship Expectation

Items	Measures	Key References
Relationship Expectation (RE1–RE5)	RE1. My information contribution will deepen the bonds between the organization's existing members and myself.	Khanam and Parveen (2019), Lee et al. (2020)
	RE2. By contributing information, I will become acquainted with new members of the organization.	
	RE3. My provision of information will broaden the breadth of my relationship with other organization members.	
	RE4. In the future, my information supply will attract easy cooperation from exceptional members.	
	RE5. My input of information will foster strong bonds among members who share common interests in the organization.	

4.2.3 Measurement of Work Engagement

Work engagement has nine items (items for each construct), and this scale is modified from the studies of Kuok and Taormina (2017), Saks (2006), Macey and Schneider (2008), and Rich et al. (2010), as shown in Table 6.

Table 6. Measurement of Work Engagement

Items	Measures	Key References
Work Engagement (WE1–WE9)	*Cognitive Work Engagement	Saks (2006), Macey and Schneider (2008), Rich et al. (2010), Kuok and Taormina (2017)
	1. My mind is often full of ideas about my work.	
	2. Wherever I am, things happen that often remind me of my work.	
	3. My mind is fully engaged with my work.	
	*Emotional Work Engagement	
	4. I feel very delighted about what I am doing whenever I am working.	
	5. I am very eager to do my work.	
	6. I feel very happy when I am carrying out my responsibilities at work.	
	*Physical Work Engagement	
	7. No matter how much I work, I have a high level of energy.	
	8. I have a great deal of stamina for my work.	
	9. I always have a lot of energy for my work.	

4.2.4 Measurement of Information Contribution Intention

The scale for information contribution intention has four items derived from Bock et al. (2005), Imlawi and Gregg (2020), and Castaneda and Durán's (2018) scales, as shown in Table 7.

Table 7. Measurement of Information Contribution Intention

Items	Measures	Key References
Information Contribution Intention (ICI1–ICI4)	ICI1. If given the opportunity, I would contribute my work experiences to coworkers.	Bock et al. (2005), Imlawi and Gregg (2020), Castaneda and Durán (2018)
	ICI2. If given the opportunity, I would contribute my ideas to coworkers.	
	ICI3. If given the opportunity, I would contribute my documents to coworkers.	
	ICI4. If given the opportunity, I would contribute specific information and knowledge gained during training to my colleagues.	

4.2.5 Measurement of Information Contribution Behavior

With the scale of information contribution behavior at work, it should be noted that, regarding mutually dependent work groups within an organization, information contribution behavior may be placed along two different dimensions: (i) among the employees, and (ii) through the organization's information platform. From the viewpoint of employees, each of these dimensions can refer to either (a) the interpersonal or (b) the organizational, thereby providing a twofold classification. There are four items for information contribution behavior, drawn from the work of Castaneda and Durán (2018), as shown in Table 8.

Table 8. Measurement of Information Contribution Behavior

Items	Measures	Key References
Information Contribution Behavior (ICB1–ICB4)	ICB1. Today, I contributed my work experiences to colleagues to enrich their work.	Castaneda and Durán (2018)
	ICB2. Today, I contributed some ideas to my colleagues to improve their work.	
	ICB3. Today, I contributed documents to my colleagues, which may be useful to them.	
	ICB4. Today, I contributed specific information that I learned in training activities to my colleagues.	

Chapter 5

V. Data Analysis and Results

5.1 Survey Administration and Sampling

I selected data for analysis in order to provide an empirical grounding for the research model and hypotheses testing. The elements in the questionnaire are based on the literature on information contribution and measured using a five-point Likert scale. My aim is to predicate the aspects that affect information contribution behavior within the organization.

To build my study model, I distributed online surveys to a sample of SMEs in China for data collection. The URL to answer the questionnaire was added to an organization-based research form that was sent to the respondents. The link contained a thorough introduction of the research objectives and that participation was completely voluntary and confidential. However, the participants who were organization members also have information contribution experience in the organization which is a limitation.

Six hundred questionnaires were sent in total, 560 participants responded, and 531 valid questionnaires were collected. The items were measured on a scale ranging from strongly agree (5), agree (4), neutral (3), disagree (2), to strongly disagree (1).

In the following section, I explain the characteristics of the participants. The direction of the correlations among variables are determined using the SPSS and AMOS. Data analysis skills are collected, followed by a discussion of the outcomes of the evaluation of the measurement model. Finally, the outcomes based on the structural model evaluation and testable hypotheses are presented.

5.2 Data Analysis

The characteristics of the respondents are shown in Tables 9-1 and 9-2, and included the age, gender, position, education, types of organization, and information contribution experience. These data are examined using frequencies tables. The data show that 46.14 percent of respondents are male and 53.86 percent are female. From the perspective of age, position, and work experience, most respondents were 21–29 years old (217, 40.87%), employees accounted for the largest proportion of position (277, 52.17%), and most respondents had a work experience of fewer than 5 years (149, 28.06% for <1 year; 142, 26.74% for 1–5 years). Four types of

SMEs were surveyed: manufacturing (156, 29.38%), wholesale (77, 14.50%), retail (92, 17.33%), and service (206, 38.79%). These data are representative of China's SMEs.

Table 9-1. Profile of Respondents

Measure	Items	Freq.	Percentage
Gender	Male	245	46.14%
	Female	286	53.86%
Age	< 20	28	5.27%
	21–29	217	40.87%
	30–39	156	29.38%
	40–49	77	14.50%
	50–59	35	6.59%
	> 60	18	3.39%
Position	Intern	124	23.35%
	Employee	277	52.17%
	Assistant manager	31	5.84%
	Manager	56	10.55%
	Senior manager	21	3.95%
	Director	11	2.07%
	CEO	11	2.07%
Annual Revenue of SMEs	< 0.5 million	75	14.12%
	0.5–1 million	78	14.69%
	1–3 million	54	10.17%
	3–5 million	46	8.66%
	5–10 million	24	4.52%
	10–30 million	56	10.55%
	30–50 million	44	8.29%
	50–100 million	61	11.49%
	100–500 million	36	6.78%
	> 500 million	57	10.73%

Table 9-2. Profile of Respondents

Measure	Items	Freq.	Percentage
Work Experience (in years)	< 1 Year	149	28.06%
	1–5 Years	142	26.74%
	5–10 Years	90	16.95%
	10–15 Years	100	18.83%
	15–20 Years	26	4.90%
	> 20 Years	24	4.52%
Education	Below high school	40	7.53%
	High school	62	11.68%
	College (2 years)	120	22.60%
	University (4 years)	242	45.57%
	Graduate	67	12.62%
Number of Employees	< 5	42	7.91%
	5–9	47	8.85%
	10–19	90	16.95%
	20– 49	59	11.11%
	50–99	72	13.56%
	100–199	60	11.30%
	200–399	63	11.86%
	> 500	98	18.46%
Types of Industry	① Manufacturing	156	29.38%
	② Wholesale	77	14.50%
	③ Retail	92	17.33%
	④ Service	206	38.79%

5.2.1 Assessment of Reliability and Validity

I now assess the measurement model for reliability and validity, followed by structural model tests to test the hypotheses. Cronbach's alpha and Fornell's composite reliability are used to assess construct reliability (Fornell and Larcker 1981). Cronbach's alpha is also used to assess the reliability of the dimensions in this study. George and Mallery (1999) contend that there is no universal interpretation of acceptable alpha values. However, according to the rule of thumb, the acceptable values range from 0.50 to 0.90, with values lower than 0.50 being unacceptable. Nunnally and Bernstein (1994) also claim that a reliability value of 0.50 to 0.60 is adequate, but a higher Cronbach's alpha is preferred. In this study, the Cronbach's alpha values for all constructions range from 0.749 to 0.884, greater than the proposed minimal cutoff of 0.50, as shown in Table 10.

Table 10. Discriminate Reliability

Items	Measures	Cronbach's Alpha
Performance Expectation (PE)	PE1, PE2, PE3, PE4, PE5	0.786
Relationship Expectation (RE)	RE1, RE2, RE3, RE4, RE5	0.749
Work Engagement (WE)	WE1, WE2, WE3, WE4, WE5, WE6, WE7, WE8, WE9	0.884
Information Contribution Intention (ICI)	ICI1, CIC2, ICI3, ICI4	0.751
Information Contribution Behavior (ICB)	ICB1, ICB2, ICB3, ICB4	0.755

Next, I perform a confirmatory factor analysis (CFA) on the model data. Hair et al. (2010) consider variables with estimates greater than 0.30 to be significant, with estimates greater than 0.40 to be more indispensable, and with estimates greater than or equal to 0.50 to be significant. A generally acceptable estimate of 0.50 or above is used as the general criterion for this study. As shown in Table 11, the estimates for all variables are greater than 0.5. The estimates of PE range from 0.702 to 0.584, the estimates of RE from 0.587 to 0.644, the estimates of WE from 0.597 to 0.693, the estimates of ICI from 0.677 to 0.650, and the estimates of ICB from 0.598 to 0.707. Therefore, all elements of this variable are retained for further analysis. CFA determines whether the metric is sufficient enough to analyze the elements and the distributions. I determine the maximum likelihood assessment to evaluate the CFA model. I then apply the SSPS and AMOS for research analysis.

Table 11. Results of Confirmatory Factor Analysis

Measures Items			Estimate	Average Variance Extracted (> 0.5)	Composite Reliability (> 0.7)
PE5	←	PE	0.584		
PE4	←	PE	0.690		
PE3	←	PE	0.636	0.599	0.882
PE2	←	PE	0.644		
PE1	←	PE	0.702		
RE5	←	RE	0.644		
RE4	←	RE	0.587		
RE3	←	RE	0.614	0.553	0.861
RE2	←	RE	0.623		
RE1	←	RE	0.587		
WE5	←	WE	0.684		
WE4	←	WE	0.676		
WE3	←	WE	0.740		
WE2	←	WE	0.640		
WE1	←	WE	0.597	0.639	0.941
WE6	←	WE	0.691		
WE7	←	WE	0.648		
WE8	←	WE	0.725		
WE9	←	WE	0.693		
ICI4	←	ICI	0.650		
ICI3	←	ICI	0.637	0.608	0.862
ICI2	←	ICI	0.660		
ICI1	←	ICI	0.677		

ICB4	←	ICB	0.707		
ICB3	←	ICB	0.704	0.609	0.861
ICB2	←	ICB	0.633		
ICB1	←	ICB	0.598		

Note: Performance Expectations (PE); Relationship Expectations (RE); Work Engagement (WE); Information Contribution Intention (ICI); Information Contribution Behavior (ICB); Composite Reliability (CR); Average Variance Extracted (AVE)

Fornell and Larcker (1981) state that the acceptable limits for compound reliability (CR) and average variance extracted (AVE) for ensuring validity are > 0.70 and > 0.50, respectively. In this study, all variables have convergent validity, with CR and AVE greater than 0.70 and 0.50, respectively. The variable values are as follows: $CR = 0.882$; $AVE = 0.599$ for PE, $CR = 0.861$; $AVE = 0.553$ for RE, $CR = 0.941$; $AVE = 0.639$ for WE, $CR = 0.862$; $AVE = 0.608$ for ICI, and $CR = 0.861$; $AVE = 0.609$ for ICB. These variables all meet the criterion of discriminant validity and the correlation value among structures (see Table 11).

Correlation analysis is used to better understand the relationship between the measured variables in the structural model. Simultaneously, to ensure the structural model's validity, it is necessary to detect whether there are obvious differences among the measured variables. That is, the discriminant validity among the measured variables must be ensured.

The usual test of discriminant validity is to compare the AVE value of a measured variable with the correlation coefficient between that variable and the other variables. When the value of the square root of the AVE of a measured variable is greater than the correlation coefficient between the variable and other variables, the measured variable has good discriminant validity.

The square root value of AVE of PE is 0.774, and the correlation coefficient values of PE and RE, WE, ICI, and ICB are 0.044, 0.024, 0.037, and 0.031, respectively. The square root value of AVE of RE is 0.744, and the correlation coefficient values of RE and WE, ICI, and ICB are 0.062, 0.057, and 0.073, respectively. The square root value of AVE of WE is 0.799, the correlation coefficient values of WE and ICI, ICB is 0.096, and 0.096, respectively, the square root value of AVE of ICI is 0.780, and the correlation coefficient value of ICI and ICB is 0.102.

The findings reveal that the square root value of the AVE of each measured variable is greater than the correlation coefficient between the measured variable and the other variables. As a result, the measurement variables in the research model have high discriminant validity (see Table 12).

The correlation coefficient reflects the relationship among variables; all correlation values of performance expectations, relationship expectations, work engagement, and information contribution intention and the dependent variable information contribution behavior are significant at the 0.001 level (p < 0.001).

Table 12. Discriminate Validity

Measures Items	PE	RE	WE	ICI	ICB	Average Variance Extracted	Composite Reliability
PE	0.774					0.599	0.882
RE	0.044	0.744				0.553	0.861
WE	0.024	0.062	0.799			0.639	0.941
ICI	0.037	0.057	0.096	0.780		0.608	0.862
ICB	0.031	0.073	0.096	0.102	0.780	0.609	0.861

Note: Performance Expectations (PE); Relationship Expectations (RE); Work Engagement (WE); Information Contribution Intention (ICI); Information Contribution Behavior (ICB); Composite Reliability (CR); Average Variance Extracted (AVE); The shaded numbers in the diagonal row are square roots of the average variance extracted.

5.2.3 Path Analysis

Table 13 shows that all of the required fit index values are within the approved range. The value of χ^2/d.f. is acceptable up to 3, and is 1.548 in the measurement model, with the root mean square error of approximation (RMSEA) value of 0.032. The root mean square residual (RMR), goodness-of-fit index (GFI), adjusted goodness-of-fit index (AGFI), parsimony goodness-of-fit index (PGFI), normed fit index (NFI), relative fit index (RFI), Tucker–Lewis index (TLI), comparative fit index (CFI), and probability (p) of close fit (PCLOSE) have values of 0.034 (< 0.05), 0.937 (> 0.9), 0.925 (> 0.9), 0.784 (high value results), 0.893 (> 0.8), 0.881 (> 0.8), 0.955 (> 0.9), 0.959 (> 0.9), and 1.000 (> 0.05), respectively. All the resultant values are significant and above the required range, indicating good fit of the model.

Table 13. Goodness of Fit Indices

Measurement Items	Description and Explanation	Scope	Fit Standard	Test Result Value
CMIN(x^2)			Lower value (< 3)	1.548
GFI		0–1	> 0.9	0.937
RMR / SRMR	Additional interpretation of x^2	0–1	< 0.05	0.034
RMSEA		0–1	< 0.05	0.032
NFI		0–1	> 0.9	0.893
RFI		0–1	> 0.9	0.881
CFI		0–1	> 0.9	0.959
LTI(NNFI)		0–1	> 0.9	0.955
AGFI		0–1	> 0.9	0.925
PNFI	Comparison between two models	0–1	Higher value	
PCFI	Comparison between two models	0–1	Higher value	
PGFI	Comparison between two models	0–1	Higher value	0.784

| AIC | Comparison between two models | | Higher value | |
| PCLOSE | | | > 0.05 | 1.000 |

Table 14 shows all of the standardized estimated values. Evidently, all factor loadings are significant at $p < .001$ and above the acceptable threshold values (the p values of PE $\rightarrow$ WE and PE $\rightarrow$ ICB are not significantly affected). The results indicate that the variable paths in the structural equation model are important for all theoretical relationships.

Table 14. Results of Path Analysis

Measures Items			Estimate	S.E.	C.R.	P
ICI	$\leftarrow$	PE	0.165	0.065	2.931	0.003**
WE	$\leftarrow$	PE	0.090	0.064	1.794	0.073
ICI	$\leftarrow$	RE	0.296	0.062	4.871	***
WE	$\leftarrow$	RE	0.323	0.064	5.674	***
ICB	$\leftarrow$	ICI	0.287	0.056	4.557	***
ICB	$\leftarrow$	PE	0.033	0.054	0.619	0.536
ICB	$\leftarrow$	RE	0.159	0.057	2.542	0.011**
ICB	$\leftarrow$	WE	0.270	0.046	4.730	***

Note: Note: *P < .05, **P < .01, ***P < .001; Critical Ratio (C.R.)

In this study, I examine the effect of performance expectation and relationship expectation on information contribution behavior through work engagement and information contribution intention by using structural equation modeling (SME).

The results of path analysis show that performance expectation has a significant direct effect on information contribution intention ($\beta = 0.165$; $p < 0.01$), supporting H2. It also has an insignificant effect on work engagement and information contribution behavior, rejecting H3 and H4. A positive relationship between information contribution intention and information contribution behavior ($\beta = 0.287$; $p < 0.001$) is confirmed, supporting H1. Further, relationship expectation positively influences information contribution intention ($\beta = 0.296$; $p < 0.001$) and information contribution behavior ($\beta = 0.159$; $p < 0.01$), supporting H8 and H7. Work engagement and information contribution behavior are also positively related ($\beta = 0.270$; $p < 0.001$), supporting H5. Finally, relationship expectation has a significant direct effect on work engagement ($\beta = 0.323$; $p < 0.001$), supporting H6. Overall, H1, H2, H5, H6, H7, and H8 are supported (see Table 14). Figure 3 illustrates the results of hypotheses testing.

Figure 3. Results of Hypotheses Testing

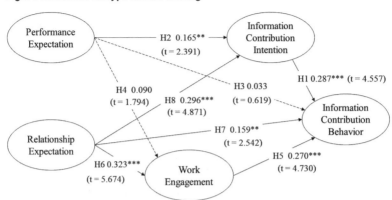

Note: Note: *P < .05, **P < .01, ***P < .001

5.2.4 Mediating Effect Analysis

A multiple mediator model is a model in which there are multiple mediator variables. These models can analyze specific, total, and contrastive mediation effects, and are divided into single-step and multiple-step models (Hayes 2009).

The multiple mediation model has three advantages over the simple mediation model. First, it allows us to obtain the total mediation effect. Second, it makes it possible to control for the specific mediating effects of other mediating variables. Third, it allows us to obtain the comparative mediation effect, which helps us judge which of the multiple mediating variable theories is more meaningful. These advantages make the use of multiple mediation models more theoretical and practical (Preacher and Hayes 2008).

However, the multiple mediation effect analysis offers only an incomplete analysis and is subject to the limitations of Sobel's test; that is, the Sobel's test statistic is complicated to calculate and needs to be calculated manually. Cheung (2007) proposes adding auxiliary variables to the SEM to conduct a complete analysis of multiple mediation effects and overcome the aforementioned limitation. The auxiliary variable is a latent variable with a variance of 0 because of which the newly added auxiliary variable in the multiple mediation model will not affect the estimated value of the original parameter and the fitting degree of the model. Hence, the auxiliary variable is also called the phantom variable (Cheung 2007; Macho and Le-dermann 2011).

Mediators play an important role in psychological, educational, social, and management research. If the independent variable "X" has a certain influence on the dependent variable "Y" through a certain variable "M," then "M" is called the mediating variable between "X" and "Y" or "M" plays a mediating role between "X" and "Y." The significance of mediation research is to help us explain the mechanism of the relationship between the independent and dependent variables, and to integrate the relationship among existing variables (Williams and MacKinnon 2008). In psychology research, the relationship among variables is rarely direct, and indirect effects are more common. Many independent psychological variables can influence the dependent variable through mediator variables.

Based on this study's research model, I hypothesize that, if the independent variable of performance expectation has a certain influence on the dependent variable of information contribution behavior through information contribution intention and work engagement, then information contribution intention and work engagement are in the independent variable of performance expectation and cause the variable of information contribution behavior to play a mediating role.

Next, I perform the mediation effects analysis with the phantom variables tool. In Table 15, the data show that, from the perspective of the total effect, PE → ICB (0.107) has an insignificant effect and RE → ICB (0.301; $p = 0.004$; $p < 0.01$) has a significant effect.

Further, the results of the direct effect and the total effect are similar, where PE → ICB (0.034) has an insignificant effect and RE → ICB (0.145; $p = 0.030$; $p < 0.05$) has a significant effect.

Finally, I illustrate the mediation effect, where PE → ICI → ICB (0.049; $p = 0.012$; $p < 0.05$) has a significant effect; PE → WE → ICB (0.025) has an insignificant effect; RE → ICI → ICB (0.077; $p = 0.004$; $p < 0.01$) has a higher significant effect; and RE → ICI → ICB (0.079; $p = 0.004$; $p < 0.01$) has a higher significant effect. The analysis shows that the designed mediators (information contribution intention and work engagement) have acceptable mediating effects.

Table 15. Results of Mediation Effect Analysis

Measures Items		Effect	S.E.	p
Total Effect	PE → ICB	0.107	0.067	0.104
	RE → ICB	0.301	0.069	**
Direct Effect	PE →ICB	0.034	0.059	0.613
	RE → ICB	0.145	0.067	0.03*
Indirect Effect	PE →ICI → ICB	0.049	0.023	0.012*
	PE →WE → ICB	0.025	0.019	0.124
	RE →ICI → ICB	0.077	0.027	**
	RE →WE → ICB	0.079	0.024	**

Note: *P < .05, **P < .01, ***P < .001

Figure 4. Results of Hypotheses Testing (Mediation Effect)

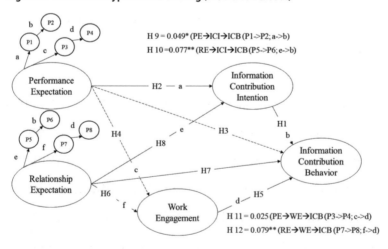

Note: *P < .05, **P < .01, ***P < .001

5.3 Hypotheses Testing Results

The outcomes of the hypotheses testing support nine of the 12 posited relationships. Table 16 summarizes the results thereof.

Table 16. Hypotheses Testing Results

Items	Hypothesis	Results
Hypothesis 1	Information contribution intention has a positive effect on information contribution behavior.	Supported
Hypothesis 2	Performance expectation has a positive effect on information contribution intention.	Supported
Hypothesis 3	Performance expectation has a positive effect on information contribution behavior.	*Not Supported*
Hypothesis 4	Performance expectation has a positive effect on work engagement.	*Not Supported*
Hypothesis 5	Work engagement has a positive effect on information contribution behavior.	Supported
Hypothesis 6	Relationship expectation has a positive effect on work engagement.	Supported
Hypothesis 7	Relationship expectation has a positive effect on information contribution intention.	Supported
Hypothesis 8	Relationship expectation has a positive effect on information contribution behavior.	Supported
Hypothesis 9	Performance expectation indirectly affects information contribution behavior through information contribution intention.	Supported
Hypothesis 10	Relationship expectation indirectly affects information contribution behavior through information contribution intention.	Supported

Hypothesis 11	Performance expectation indirectly affects information contribution behavior through work engagement.	*Not Supported*
Hypothesis 12	Relationship expectation indirectly affects information contribution behavior through work engagement.	Supported

The results of the structural model analyses are summarized as follows:

First, regarding performance expectation, the following results from H1 to H3 are obtained:

Hypothesis 1: Information contribution intention has a positive effect on information contribution behavior.

Hypothesis 2: Performance expectation has a positive effect on information contribution intention.

Hypothesis 3: Performance expectation has a positive effect on information contribution behavior (not supported).

The positive effect of performance expectations on information contribution intentions is confirmed. At the same time, information contribution intention is confirmed to have a positive effect on information contribution behavior. However, the direct effect of performance expectations on information contribution behavior is not supported.

Second, regarding relationship expectation, the following results from H6 to H8 are obtained:

Hypothesis 6: Relationship expectation has a positive effect on work engagement.

Hypothesis 7: Relationship expectation has a positive effect on information contribution intention.

Hypothesis 8: Relationship expectation has a positive effect on information contribution behavior.

H6, H7, and H8 are all supported, which is a satisfactory result. Performance expectation has a positive effect on work engagement, which indicates that employees' information contribution is affected by self-work engagement, which ultimately affects information contribution behavior. Moreover, the hypothesis that work engagement has a positive effect on information contribution behavior is also supported. H6, H7, and H8, which focus on the effect of relationship expectation on information contribution and work engagement, are supported. Relationship expectation has a positive effect on information contribution intention, which, in turn, has a positive effect on information contribution behavior. Relationship expectation also has a positive effect on work engagement, which, in turn, has a positive effect on information contribution behavior.

Third, regarding work engagement, H4 and H5 show that performance expectation has an insignificant effect on work engagement, which, in turn, has a positive effect on information contribution behavior.

Hypothesis 4: Performance expectation has a positive effect on work engagement (not supported).

Hypothesis 5: Work engagement has a positive effect on information contribution behavior.

Finally, regarding the mediation effect, I explain the multiple mediation model in detail, and the hypotheses results are as follows:

Hypothesis 9: Performance expectation indirectly affects information contribution behavior through information contribution intention.

Hypothesis 10: Relationship expectation indirectly affects information contribution behavior through information contribution intention.

Hypothesis 11: Performance expectation indirectly affects information contribution behavior through work engagement (not supported).

Hypothesis 12: Relationship expectation indirectly affects information contribution behavior through work engagement.

The results of the media analysis show that H9, H10, and H12 are all supported, and only H11 is not supported. It is significant that performance expectation and relationship expectation affect information contribution behavior through information contribution intention. It is also significant that relationship expectation affects information contribution behavior through work engagement. However, the mediating effect of performance expectation through work engagement was insignificant.

The hypotheses results illustrate that—

• Performance expectation positively affects the result of information contribution behavior through the mediating effect of information contribution intention.

• Relationship expectation not only directly affects information contribution behavior, but also affects information contribution behavior through the mediation of work engagement, where the mediating effect of work engagement is more significant.

• Relationship expectation has a very significant effect on information contribution compared with performance expectation.

I interpret these findings as follows. In the information contribution process of China's SMEs, both performance and relationship expectations have a meaningful effect on information contribution, but relationship expectation has a more significant effect on information contribution.

The results of the hypotheses give us a more in-depth impression of "relationship." I thus provide an in-depth interpretation of relationships and discuss the importance of relationship expectation in the context of the findings.

Guanxi, as explained, describes the relationship between individuals and business networks in China (Luo et al. 2012). Human relationships are highly valued in Chinese society and are the foundation of economic and social organization (Hwang 1987). Among individuals relationships are based on reciprocal exchanges among members of an inner circle (Hwang 1987; Fei 1992), and the motivation for obtaining personal information is to maintain interpersonal relationships or friendships (Noh and Kang 2021).

Further, relationship expectation is mediated by work engagement. This effect is also highly significant. This result reflects the importance attached by Chinese SMEs to the information contribution relationship, and is characteristic of China and the culture of Chinese corporate relations.

Ordonez de Pablos (2005) proposes that it implies the development of close relationships with others because of emotional relationships among individuals. In other words, there is an emotional connection between two different organizations; that is, *guanxi* is a very important strategic and organizational factor that constitutes an intimate and powerful network in business relationships between individuals and companies in China (Gao et al. 2014).

Knowledge sharing among organizations is inseparable from the relationship and information contribution among employees of the organization, at least in China's relational society (Gao et al. 2014). Kim and Kim (2015) further find that employee relations are related to positive attitudes, and there is a high correlation between organizational commitment and job satisfaction. According to the social exchange relationship, when two people are influenced by the social and organizational environment, especially when exchanging unspecified cooperative outputs such as knowledge, their relationship is the main factor that determines their attitude and motivation. Employees who believe that work engagement improves their reciprocal relationships with others and are driven by a desire for fairness and reciprocity are more likely to have positive attitudes and motivations toward work engagement (Huber 2001).

It is important for employees to expect a good relationship and a continuation of their relationships. A good work engagement will also promote employee information contribution, which is beneficial to the organization's performance, value, and competitiveness.

To further test the differences among groups and the fit of the model, I analyze the types of Chinese SMEs. I compare the differences among groups of different types of enterprises through a *T*-test, multi-group sample structure model analysis, path analysis, and multiple mediation analysis.

5.4 Independent *T*-Test Analysis

In the analysis section, I first perform an independent sample t-test analysis. I select two independent samples for detection and analysis. The goal is to test whether the means of the dependent variable regarding the contribution of information in the two groups are significantly different. Mean, standard deviation, t, and Sig. (two-tailed) are used to determine statistical significance.

First, I establish a return to nothing hypothesis, with no difference in the information contribution behavior of employees in Group 1 and Group 2. Second, I set the opposing hypothesis, where the information contribution behavior of employees in Group 1 (service industry) and Group 2 (non-service industry) is different. I perform an examination of equality differences through Levene's test for equality of variances.

The two groups are assumed to have equal variances if $p > 0.05$ in the Levene's test for equality of variances (indicated by significance in the figure). If $p < 0.05$ in the Levene's test for equality of variances (indicated by significance in the figure), it cannot be assumed that the two groups have equal variances. Checking the t-test for equality of means, if $p > 0.05$ in Levene's equality of variance test (represented by Sig. [two-tailed] in the figure), the null hypothesis is not rejected, indicating no significant difference between the groups. If $p < 0.05$ in the Levene variance equality test (represented by Sig. [two-tailed] in the figure), the null hypothesis is rejected, and I test the group statistics and compare the differences between the two groups of values.

The results show that there are 206 samples in Group 1 and 325 samples in Group 2; Group 1 is larger than Group 2. The mean of Group 1 is 4.070 and the mean of Group 2 is 4.180; the mean of Group 1 is higher than that of Group 2. Two-tailed significance is $0.805 > 0.05$, the p *value* of the average difference between the two groups is 0.033, and $p < 0.05$ is within the available range. The results confirm a difference in the information contribution behavior of Group 1 and Group 2, that is, between the service and non-service industries in China's SMEs (see Table 17).

Table 17. Independent Sample _T_-Test

Items	Mean		Std. Deviation		Levene's Test for Equality of Variances		_t_	_p_
Types of Industry	Group1: Service Industry (n=206)	Group2: Non-Service Industry (n=325)	Group1: Service Industry	Group2: Non-Service Industry	_F_	Sig.	2.138	0.033
	4.070	4.180	0.534	0.536	0.601	0.805		

*_p_ < 0.05, **_p_ < 0.01, ***_p_ < 0.001; Levene's test is an inferential statistic used to assess the equality of variances for a variable calculated for two or more groups (Levene and Howard 1961).

5.5 Multi-group Sample Structure Model Analysis

The analysis in subsection 5.4 yields the research path model diagram. To explore whether the path model graph is suitable for a certain group, and whether the corresponding parameters are also suitable for other groups, I perform an AMOS multi-group analysis.

The principle of multi-group analysis is to divide the original single common change structure relationship in a single sample into several parallel common change structures, and then evaluate and analyze these common change structures. After this, whether the effect of influencing factors on different populations is equivalent is ascertained. The group invariance test then tests whether the factor loadings between the latent variables corresponding to multiple groups and the indicator variables are equal, which is a test to measure the invariance of the model. I classify the types of enterprises and divide the two groups of service and non-service enterprises to explore how employees' performance and relationship expectations predict their information-contribution behavior.

Table 18-1. Multi-group Analysis Fitting Results

Model	CMIN	DF	P	CMIN/DF
Unconstrained	838.774	632.000	0.000	1.327
Measurement Weights	875.803	654.000	0.000	1.339
Structural Weights	881.278	662.000	0.000	1.331
Structural Residuals	883.152	667.000	0.000	1.324
Measurement Residuals	997.051	694.000	0.000	1.437

Table 18-2. Multiple Group Analysis Fitting Results

Model	NFI	RFI	IFI	TLI	CFI	RMR	GFI	AGFI
Unconstrained	0.833	0.815	0.953	0.947	0.952	0.038	0.898	0.878
Measurement Weights	0.826	0.813	0.949	0.945	0.949	0.039	0.895	0.878
Structural Weights	0.825	0.814	0.950	0.946	0.949	0.041	0.894	0.879
Structural Residuals	0.824	0.815	0.950	0.947	0.950	0.042	0.893	0.879
Measurement Residuals	0.802	0.800	0.930	0.929	0.930	0.043	0.883	0.873

The numerical test results of the NFI, RFI, incremental fit index (IFI), TLI, CFI, GFI, AGFI, RMSEA, AIC, and expected cross validation index (ECVI) from the multi-group analysis are shown in the adaptation table. The data are not very different, and the results show goodness of fit (see Table 18-2).

Table 19-1. Invariance Test Results

Model	delta-CMIN	delta-DF	p	delta-NFI	delta-RFI	delta-IFI	delta-CFI	delta-GFI	delta-AGFI
Measurement Weights	37.029	22.000	0.023	-0.007	-0.002	-0.004	-0.003	-0.003	0.000
Structural Weights	42.504	30.000	0.065	-0.008	-0.001	-0.003	-0.003	-0.004	0.001
Structural Residuals	44.378	35.000	0.133	-0.009	0.000	-0.003	-0.002	-0.005	0.001
Measurement Residuals	158.277	62.000	0.000	-0.031	-0.015	-0.023	-0.022	-0.015	-0.005

Table 19-1 shows that the chi-square value of the measurement weights model relative to the unconstrained model changes to 37.029 ($p = 0.023$; $p < 0.05$); the chi-square value of the structural weights model relative to the unconstrained model changes to 42.504 ($p = 0.065$; $p > 0.05$); the chi-square value of the structural residuals model relative to the unconstrained model changes to 44.378 ($p = 0.133$; $p > 0.05$); the chi-square value of the measurement residuals model relative to the unconstrained model is changes to 158.277 ($p - 0.000$; $p < 0.05$). However, the delta value shows that almost all the changes in value are less than 0.05, indicating that the changes in the measurement residuals model and unconstrained model are not obvious.

Further, the p value is greater than 0.05, confirming that the model as a whole is suitable. Although the p value in the measurement residuals model is less than 0.05, the values of delta-NFI, delta-RFI, delta-IFI, delta-CFI, delta-GFIHE, and delta-AGFI are less than 0.05. Compared with the value of the unconstrained model, the change is insignificant; hence, the model is relatively stable.

Table 19-2. Invariance Test Results

Model	AIC	ECVI
Unconstrained	1086.774	2.054
Measurement Weights	1079.803	2.041
Structural Weights	1069.278	2.021
Structural Residuals	1061.152	2.006
Measurement Residuals	1121.051	2.119

Based on the results of the invariance test, or from the adaptation index of the parsimonious model, the model with the smallest intermediate value between AIC and ECVI is the structural residuals model. This means that the most parsimonious model from the five models can be chosen. In such a case, the results confirm the structural residuals model to be the best (see Table 19-2). Analyzing the types of SMEs shows that the service and non-service industry group models are suitable for the research model.

The *T*-test analysis further reveals differences in the information contributions of employees in the SMEs of both the service and non-service industries. The multiple group model analysis confirms that the models of the service and non-service industry groups fit the research model. In the next section, I perform an analysis of the specific differences between the two groups.

5.5.1 Analysis Results of Service Industry Group Model 1

I test the service industry (Group 1) model to examine the effect of performance and relationship expectations on information contribution behavior using SEM. The path analysis results for Model 1 for the service industry group show that $RE \rightarrow ICI$ ($\beta = 0.378$; $p < 0.001$); $RE \rightarrow WE$ ($\beta = 0.380$; $p < 0.001$); $RE \rightarrow ICB$ ($\beta = 0.202$; $p < 0.05$); $ICI \rightarrow ICB$ ($\beta = 0.313$; $p < 0.001$); and $WE \rightarrow ICB$ ($\beta = 0.228$; $p < 0.01$). The overall path analysis results of the model are satisfactory (see Table 20).

Table 20. Results of Path Analysis (Model 1)

Model — 1 (Service Industry Group n=206)			Estimate	S.E.	C.R.	P	Label
ICI	←	PE	0.144	0.106	1.710	0.087	b2_1
WE	←	PE	0.109	0.104	1.388	0.165	b4_1
ICI	←	RE	0.378	0.107	4.070	***	b5_1
WE	←	RE	0.380	0.109	4.214	***	b7_1
ICB	←	ICI	0.313	0.092	3.408	***	b1_1
ICB	←	PE	0.120	0.101	1.506	0.132	b3_1
ICB	←	RE	0.202	0.112	2.078	0.038*	b6_1
ICB	←	WE	0.228	0.080	2.716	0.007**	b8_1

Note: $*P < .05$, $**P < .01$, $***P < .001$; Critical Ratio (C.R.)

Thus, performance expectation had no significant direct effect on information contribution intention ($t = 1.710$; $t < 1.95$), no significant direct effect on work engagement ($t = 1.388$, $t < 1.95$), and no significant direct effect on information contribution behavior ($t = 1.506$, $t < 1.95$). Further, there exists a positive correlation between relationship expectation and information contribution intention ($\beta = 0.378$; $p < 0.001$; $t = 4.070$; $t > 1.95$) and between information contribution intention and information contribution behavior ($\beta = 0.313$; $p < 0.001$; $t = 3.408$; $t > 1.95$). There exists a weak positive correlation between relationship expectation and information contribution behavior ($\beta = 0.202$; $p < 0.05$; $t = 2.078$; $t > 1.95$).

Further, work engagement and information contribution behavior are positively correlated ($\beta = 0.228$; $p < 0.01$; $t = 2.716$; $t > 1.95$). Relationship expectation has a significant direct effect on work engagement ($\beta = 0.380$; $p < 0.001$; $t = 4.214$; $t > 1.95$), but a weak positive correlation with information contribution behavior ($\beta = 0.202$; $p < 0.05$; $t = 2.078$; $t > 1.95$) (see Figure 5). Thus, model analysis reveals that employees of service SMEs pay more attention to relationship expectation when contributing information to the organization.

Figure 5. Multiple Group Analysis Service Industry Group 1

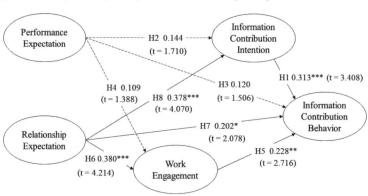

Note: Standardized estimates Service Industry Group; Unconstrained CMIN/ DF=1.327; p=0.000; RMR=0.038; RMSEA=0.025; IFI=0.953; CFI=0.952

Table 21. Results of Mediation Effect Analysis (Model 1)

Measures Items		Effect	S.E.	p
Total Effect	PE → ICB	0.043	0.073	0.543
	RE → ICB	0.254	0.080	**
Direct Effect	PE → ICB	-0.030	0.066	0.660
	RE → ICB	0.097	0.076	0.180
Indirect Effect	PE →ICI → ICB	0.051	0.024	0.011*
	PE →WE → ICB	0.023	0.017	0.185
	RE →ICI → ICB	0.082**	0.029	**
	RE →WE →ICB	0.075**	0.024	**

Note: *P < .05, **P < .01, ***P < .001

Figure 6. Results of Hypotheses Testing (Mediation Effect of Model 1)

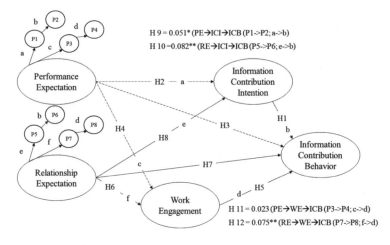

Based on the service industry Group 1 model, I apply a multiple mediation model and perform a mediation effect analysis with the phantom variable tool. In Table 21, the data show that, first, from the perspective of the total effect, PE → ICB (0.043) has an insignificant effect and RE → ICB (0.254; p=0.004; $p < 0.01$) has a significant effect. Second, in the direct effects, PE → ICB (-0.030) and RE → ICB (0.097) have an insignificant effect. Finally, in the mediation effect, PE → ICI → ICB (0.051; $p = 0.011$; $p < 0.05$) has a significant effect; PE → WE → ICB (0.023) has an insignificant effect; RE → ICI → ICB (0.082; $p = 0.004$; $p < 0.01$) has a higher significant effect; and RE → WE → ICB (0.075; $p = 0.004$; $p < 0.01$) has a higher significant effect. The multiple mediation model of the service industry group shows that the mediating factors designed (information contribution intention and work engagement) in this study have an acceptable mediating effect.

The results of the hypotheses help to construct the model results. The service industry group model shows that performance expectation positively affects information contribution behavior through the mediation of information contribution intention. This result is not significant, and relationship expectation not only directly affects information contribution behavior, but also affects it through work engagement. The degree of mediation affects information contribution behavior, and the mediating effect of work engagement is more significant. Further, relationship expectation has a highly significant effect on information contribution compared with performance expectation.

The results of the model data confirm that when employees in the service industry group of China's SMEs contribute information, the relationship expectation is more significant and its mediating effect through work engagement is also very significant. Thus, these employees pay more attention to the relationship during information contribution. This makes it important for them to expect good and continuous relationship management.

5.5.2 Analysis Results of Non-service Industry Group Model 2

Next, I test the non-service industry Group 2 model and examine the effect of performance and relationship expectations on information contribution behavior using SEM. The path analysis results show that $PE \rightarrow ICI$ ($\beta = 0.174$; $p < 0.05$); $RE \rightarrow ICI$ ($\beta = 0.229$; $p < 0.01$; $RE \rightarrow WE$ ($\beta = 0.283$; $p < 0.001$); $ICI \rightarrow ICB$ ($\beta = 0.288$; $p < 0.001$); and $WE \rightarrow ICB$ ($\beta = 0.268$; $p < 0.001$). The overall path analysis results for the model are satisfactory (see Table 22).

Table 22. Results of Path Analysis (Model 2)

Model — 2 (Non-Service Industry Group n=325)		Estimate	S.E.	C.R.	P	Label
ICI	← PE	0.174	0.080	2.321	0.020*	b2_2
WE	← PE	0.072	0.081	1.100	0.271	b4_2
ICI	← RE	0.229	0.074	2.876	0.004**	b5_2
WE	← RE	0.283	0.079	3.860	***	b7_2
ICB	← ICI	0.288	0.071	3.385	***	b1_2
ICB	← PE	-0.028	0.062	-0.395	0.693	b3_2
ICB	← RE	0.139	0.061	1.742	0.082	b6_2
ICB	← WE	0.268	0.054	3.560	***	b8_2

Note: Note: *$P < .05$, **$P < .01$, ***$P < .001$; Critical Ratio (C.R.); Non-service industry type groups include the manufacturing industry, wholesale industry, and retail industry.

I find that performance expectation has a significant direct effect on information contribution intention ($\beta = 0.174$; $p < 0.01$; $t = 2.321$; $t < 1.95$), an insignificant direct effect on work engagement ($t = 1.100$; $t < 1.95$), and an insignificant direct effect on information contribution behavior ($t = -0.028$; $t < 1.95$), whereas information contribution intention has a direct effect on information contribution behavior ($\beta = 0.288$; $p < 0.001$; $t = 3.385$; $t > 1.95$) (see Figure 5). There exists a positive correlation between relationship expectation and information contribution intention ($\beta = 0.229$; $p < 0.05$; $t = 2.876$; $t > 1.95$) and between information contribution intention and information contribution behavior ($\beta = 0.288$; $p < 0.001$; $t = 3.385$; $t > 1.95$). However, there exists an insignificant effect between relationship expectation and information contribution behavior ($t = 1.742$; $t < 1.95$). Thus, employees in non-service SMEs pay more attention to performance expectation when contributing information. Further, work engagement and information contribution behavior are positively correlated ($\beta = 0.268$; $p < 0.05$; $t = 3.560$; $t > 1.95$), whereas relationship expectation has a significant direct effect on work engagement ($\beta = 0.283$; $p < 0.001$; $t = 3.860$; $t > 1.95$).

Figure 7. Multiple Group Analysis for Non-Service Industry Group 2 Model

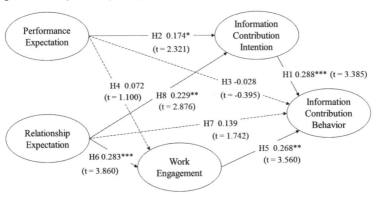

Note: *Standardized estimates Non-Service Industry Group; Unconstrained CMIN/DF=1.327; p=0.000; RMR=0.038; RMSEA=0.025; IFI=0.953; CFI=0.952*

Table 23. Results of Mediation Effect Analysis (Model 2)

Measures Items		Effect	S.E.	p
Total Effect	PE → ICB	0.230	0.112	0.041*
	RE → ICB	0.404	0.130	**
Direct Effect	PE → ICB	0.157	0.106	0.146
	RE → ICB	0.247	0.129	0.043*
Indirect Effect	PE →ICI → ICB	0.051	0.024	0.011*
	PE →WE → ICB	0.023	0.017	0.185
	RE →ICI → ICB	0.082	0.029	**
	RE →WE →ICB	0.075	0.024	**

Figure 8. Results of Hypotheses Testing (Mediation Effect of Model 2)

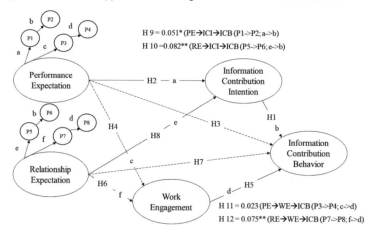

Next, I apply a multiple mediation model and analyze the mediation effect through the phantom variable tool. In Table 23, the data show that, first, from the perspective of the total effect, PE → ICB (0.230; $p = 0.041$; $p < 0.05$) and RE → ICB (0.404; p=0.004;

$p < 0.01$) have a significant effect. That is, both performance and relationship expectations have a significant direct effect on information contribution behavior. Second, in the direct effects, PE → ICB (0.157) has no significant effect and RE → ICB (0.247; p = 0.043; $p < 0.05$) has a significant effect. Thus, both performance and relationship expectations have an insignificant effect on information contribution behavior. Finally, in the mediation effect, PE → ICI → ICB (0.051; p = 0.011; $p < 0.05$) has a significant effect; PE → WE → ICB (0.023) has no significant effect; RE → ICI → ICB (0.082; p = 0.004; $p < 0.01$) has a higher significant effect; and RE → WE → ICB (0.075; p = 0.004; $p < 0.01$) has a higher significant effect. Thus, the mediating factors designed (information contribution intention and work engagement) have acceptable mediating effects.

The results of the hypotheses help to construct the model results. The model for the non-service industry group shows that performance expectation positively affects information contribution behavior through the mediation of information contribution intention, and that the results are significant. Further, relationship expectation affects information contribution behavior through the mediation of work engagement, and this mediating effect is more significant.

The results of the model data confirm that during information contribution among non-service SMEs, performance expectation has a more significant effect on information contribution, and its mediation effect through information contribution intention is also very significant. Thus, these employees pay more attention to performance when they contribute information, and it is very important for them to expect organizational performance. Relationship expectation also has some influence on information contribution in this group, and it mediates the promotion of information contribution through work engagement.

In conclusion, performance expectation affects information contribution, which is the difference between non-service and service industry groups. Improving production and organizational performance in the enterprise is the main characteristic of non-service industry groups.

5.5.3 Comparative Analysis Results of Model 1 and Model 2

In the final part of this analysis, I compare the path results of the service industry Group 1 model and non-service industry Group 2 model. I first articulate their similarities: relationship expectation affects information contribution behavior through the mediation of work engagement, and this mediating effect is very significant. Relationship expectation affects information contribution behavior through the mediation of information contribution intention, and the mediating effect of work engagement is very significant. Relationship expectation has a very significant effect on information contribution compared with performance expectation. Both service and non-service SME employees show concern for relationships when they contribute information, and good work engagement consistently mediates the influence of information contribution behavior.

Regarding group differences, I find the following. In the service industry, relationships are built through interactions between suppliers and consumers, and value is generated through this relationship. Put differently, humans realize value through the creation of intangible commodities (i.e., relationships), where all objects and all humans have meaning (Kim 2017). In the world of tangible goods, products and services are core, but in service-oriented logic, where intangible goods reign supreme, services and experiences are core. As the foundation of sustainable growth is the relationship, this relationship presupposes a two-way association between service providers and consumers than the conventional unidirectional association. Therefore, this relationship is also the essence of the human world and the natural world (Kim 2018).

Byun and Kim (2020) state that relationships are the most important feature in human history. Humans are relational animals who impart value. *Things* are only given meaning through their relationship with humans. In service economies, the relationship is especially important because, even if the customer dislikes a product, he/she considers the attitude of the service provider to continue the relationship.

Ahn and Lee (2000) also argue that building long-term relationships with customers is the most effective strategy for gaining competitive advantages; Kim (2017) lends credence to this finding by confirming that strong relationships with customers lead to a higher likelihood of revisits and referrals. Similarly, Kim and Kim (2015) find that employee relationships are related to positive attitudes, and there is a high correlation between organizational commitment and job satisfaction. Note that job satisfaction and commitment are also related to job performance (Li 2015).

The service industry group model shows that performance expectation positively affects the information contribution behavior through the mediating effect of information contribution intention, but this result is not significant. Yet, it is significant that relationship expectation not only directly affects information contribution behaviors, but also influences the results of information contribution behavior through the mediating effect of work engagement.

The results also verify the importance and relevance of relationship expectation to employee information contribution in the service industry. In this study, there are two major categories of industries. Among them, non-service industries include manufacturing, wholesale, and retail, and I focus on manufacturing. The economic development of each country is inseparable from the joint efforts of all those involved in that economy. Manufacturing, though, is foundational to economic development, and different from the service industry. Manufacturing is organized and operated with the product as the center, whereas the service industry is people centric. The former may not directly interact with customers, but the service industry is inseparable from its relationship with customers, as the service object is people. Finally, manufacturing production facilities can be distantly located from consumers, but service facilities have to be close to customers.

However, the non-service industry group model shows that performance expectation positively affects the results of information contribution behavior through the mediating effect of information contribution intention. Further, the direct effect of relationship expectation on information contribution behavior is not significant.

The significant effect of non-service industries on performance expectation is also verified. Employees in non-service industries are product centric, organize and operate enterprises by manufacturing products, and do not have direct contact with customers. In non-service industries, production and organizational performance come first.

Finally, SME employees in the service industry pay more attention to relationships when contributing information; they prioritize good and long-lasting relationships. However, when employees of non-service SMEs contribute information, they pay more attention to performance in addition to relationships. Their expectations of organizational and enterprise performance are key, along with their focus on production and organizational performance. This is the main and unique feature of the non-service industry.

Chapter 6

VI. Conclusions

6.1 Conclusions

『*Understanding Employee Information Behavior*』 This book details the influences and relational factors that affect the information contribution behavior of employees in an organization. Here we summarize the findings of this book.

The intention of providing information in an organization depends on the performance and relationship expectations of the provider. If the information provided can be helpful for the development and performance of the organization, the provider will be more willing to provide this information. However, some members of the organization provide information in seeking to improve the relationship among members.

In this study, the most important factor influencing information contribution is the relational factor that indicates the degree of ties among groups. From the perspective of expectancy theory, I explore the factors that affect the intention toward and behavior of information contribution among the employees of SMEs in China, where *guanxi*—personal connections—dictates the corporate culture among and within organizations. This is the unique context of the study. Accordingly, I construct a new information contribution model, which yields two important variables—performance expectation and relationship expectation—and includes the mediating role of work engagement.

I use SEM to test the predictive powers on the behaviors of information contribution. The findings confirm the hypothesis that performance expectation affects information contribution intention, work engagement, and information contribution behavior. The role of relationship expectation in the research model is especially examined owing to the unique characteristics of the Chinese relational culture described above.

The results confirm that relationship expectation affects an individual's work engagement, information contribution intention, and information contribution behavior. Moreover, performance and relationship expectations indirectly influence information contribution behavior via information contribution intention and work engagement.

These findings lend an important insight into evolving constructs (i.e., information contribution intention and work engagement) and how organizations can enable employee performance and relationships through work engagement. Given the importance of information contribution in SMEs—and the importance of information contribution in the future—I believe the findings herein will be useful to researchers working to improve our collective understanding of information contribution within and outside organizations.

6.2 Discussions

The complex combination of perspectives employed in this study contributes significantly to the collective understanding of why information workers may or may not choose to engage in information-contributing behavior. The following findings are particularly significant, and I offer, alongside them, some critical recommendations for information management.

First, set a performance reward mechanism within the organization, and encourage employees to make information contributions through performance completion and performance expectation. Processed information contribution is likely to promote the transfer of information within the organization and will improve organizational work efficiency, and ultimately bring employees closer to organizational performance goals.

Second, interpersonal relationships within the organization will enhance information contribution among employees and between employees and the organization, triggering a virtuous cycle of increased information sharing, improvements in relationships, and increase in performances. This two-way relationship is more accented under the influence of *guanxi* and similar cultural contexts.

Third, regulating and improving employees' work engagement will indirectly enhance their information-contribution behavior, which is a key result that was verified in the study.

Finally, the experimental design improves internal validity while decreasing external validity. This study recruited 531 SME employees from various locations in China, and the sample data revealed that a majority of them were concentrated in the southeastern coastal provinces, raising concerns about the generalizability of the results. Future research should include samples from various commercial companies and regions, as well as field study designs, to better answer the research questions.

6.3 Implications

This study contributes to the existing research on information-contributing behavior by paying particular attention to the importance of performance, relationships, and work engagement in information-contributing behavior.

The goal of this research is to gain a better understanding of the factors that influence the motivation and intentions that underpin employees' information-sharing practices. As a result, I (1) identified some potentially important motivational factors, that is, performance and relationship expectations; (2) combined these factors with expectancy theory and the TRA model; (3) modified the standard TRA formulation by designing antecedent variables and mediator variables; and (4) provided support for the standard TRA formulation and extended the TRA model.

6.4 Limitations

Even though the experimental process was meticulously planned, there may be unanticipated or even uncontrollable elements. Cultural factors, for example, could not be disregarded from the current study because the participants were Chinese. I expect the study to expand to other regions so the findings can be further validated. Given these constraints, I strongly encourage additional research based on the study's findings using more rigorous study designs and considering regional heterogeneity.

In this study, I use both work engagement and information contribution intention as mediating variables. Although the model shows that work engagement is in the front position and information contribution intention is in the back position, I did not design for the influence of the two, leaving the hypothesis thereof undeveloped. This is because I mainly study the effect of performance and relationship expectations on information contribution and the mediating effect of work engagement.

In terms of model construction and expansion, there may be some deficiencies in model verification and theoretical support, but this is also a rigorous design and innovation research, which could be valuable as a reference for model expansion and application. In future research, it is necessary to further improve the hypothesis of the mediating variable, work engagement, and provide more sufficient empirical research for the verification of the model.

6.5 Future Research

The opportunities for model extension include the following: (1) develop personal factors that affect information contribution (e.g., personal trust); (2) strengthen the effect of work engagement on information contribution intentions; (3) increase the number of moderator variables (gender, number of employees, etc.); (4) increase the number of control variables (e.g., perceived organizational support); and (4) increase the number of innovation mediator variables.

I must also recognize the importance of expanding research in future research by (1) including individuals' actual information-contribution behavior; (2) investigating the contribution of specific types of information; (3) investigating the contribution of information beyond the boundaries of a single organization (reflecting organizational boundaries); and (4) recognizing that employees contribute information either directly or indirectly through technological tools. In addition, (5) in the multi-group analysis, in addition to the types of SMEs, categories such as the number of employees, employee positions, annual income of SMEs, employee education, and geographic location of the company should be added to compare the differences among groups through multiple perspectives. This will reveal the differences in the information contribution of employees of different scales in SMEs, and ultimately guide enterprise managers to establish a reasonable management mechanism, optimize organizational management, improve organizational efficiency and performance, and promote organizational development—the ultimate goal of enterprise.

Reference

Ajzen, I., & Fishbein, M. (1975). A Bayesian analysis of attribution processes. *Psychological bulletin, 82*(2), 261.

Ajzen, I., & Fishbein, M. (1980). Understanding attitudes and predicting social ehavior. Englewood Cliffs NJ: Pren-tice Hall.

Al-Zu'bi, H. A. (2011). Organizational citizenship behavior and impacts on knowledge sharing: An empirical study. *International business research, 4*(3), 221-227.

Armitage, C. J. and Conner, M. (2001). Efficacy of the theory of planned behavior: a meta-analytic review. *Br. J. Soc. Psychol., 40*(4),471-499

Agarwal, U. A. (2014). Linking justice, trust, and innovative work behavior to work engagement. *Personnel Review.*

Agarwal, U. A., Datta, S., Blake-Beard, S., & Bhargava, S. (2012). Linking LMX, innovative work behavior and turnover intentions: The mediating role of work engagement. *Career development international.*

Andrew, O. C., & Sofian, S. (2012). Individual factors and work outcomes of employee engagement. *Procedia-Social and behavioral sciences, 40*, 498-508.

Abrahamson, E. (1991). Managerial fads and fashions: The diffusion and rejection of innovations. *Academy of management review, 16*(3), 586-612.

Alavi, M., & Leidner, D. E. (2001). Knowledge management and knowledge management systems: Conceptual foundations and research issues. *MIS quarterly*, 107-136.

Andrews, K. M., & Delahaye, B. L. (2000). Influences on knowledge processes in organizational learning: The psychosocial filter. *Journal of Management studies, 37*(6), 797-810.

Ahn, S. H. & Lee, K. H. (2000). A study on the development of long-term relationship between salesperson and customer. *Journal of the Korean Society of Clothing and Textiles, 24*(8), 1230-1241.

Byun, M., & Kim, H. (2020). A Study on the Influence of Service Nature by Service Industry on Job Performance. *The Journal of the Korea Contents Association, 20*(4), 331-347.

Blau, P. M. (1963). The dynamics of bureaucracy: Study of interpersonal relations in two government agencies, Rev.

Blau, P.M. (1964). Exchange and Power in Social Life. Wiley, New York, YN.

Barua, A., Ravindran, S., & Whinston, A. B. (2007). Enabling information sharing within organizations. *Information Technology and Management, 8*(1), 31-45.

Blau, P. M. (1967). Exchange and Power in Social Life, John New York.

Blatt, R., Christianson, M.K., Sutcliffe, K.M. and Rosenthal, M.M. (2006), "A sensemaking lens on reliability", *Journal of Organizational Behavior, 27*(7), 897-917.

Bock, G.W., Kim, Y.G., 2002. Breaking the myths of rewards: an exploratory study of attitudes about knowledge sharing. *Information Resources Management Journal 15*(2), 14-21.

Bock, G., Zmud, R., Kim, Y. and Lee, J. (2005). Behavioral intention formation in knowledge sharing: examining the roles of extrinsic motivators, social-psychological forces, and organizational climate. *MIS Quarterly, 29*(1), 87-111.

Baird, L., & Henderson, J. C. (2001). *The knowledge engine: How to create fast cycles of knowledge-to-performance and performance-to-knowledge.* Berrett-Koehler Publishers.

Barnes, S. B. (2001). Online connections: Internet interpersonal relationships. Hampton Press, Incorporated.

Bandura, A. (1997). Self-efficacy: The exercise of control. New York: Freeman.

Burt, R. S. (1997). "The Contingent Value of Social Capital." *Administrative Science Quarterly, 42*(2), 339-365.

Blau, P. (1967). Exchange and Power in Social Life. New York: Wiley

Bailey, C., Madden, A., Alfes, K., & Fletcher, L. (2017). The meaning, antecedents, and outcomes of employee engagement: A narrative synthesis. *International Journal of Management Reviews, 19*(1), 31-53.

Coetsee, L. D. (2003). Peak performance and productivity. *Potchefstroom: Van Schaik.*

Chow, W. S., & Chan, L. S. (2008). Social network, social trust, and shared goals in organizational knowledge sharing. *Information & management, 45*(7), 458-465.

Cabrera, A., & Cabrera, E. F. (2002). Knowledge-sharing dilemmas. *Organi-*

zation studies, 23(5), 687-710.

Chiu, C. M., Hsu, M. H., & Wang, E. T. (2006). Understanding knowledge sharing in virtual communities: An integration of social capital and social cognitive theories. *Decision support systems, 42*(3), 1872-1888.

Constant, D., Kiesler, S., & Sproull, L. (1994). What's mine is ours, or is it? A study of attitudes about information sharing. *Information systems research, 5*(4), 400-421.

Compeau, D.R., Higgins, C.A., (1995). Computer self-efficacy development of a measure and initial test. *MIS Quarterly, 19*(2), 189-211.

Castaneda, D. I., Ríos, M. F., & Durán, W. F. (2016). Determinants of knowledge-sharing intention and knowledge-sharing behavior in a public organization. *Knowledge Management & E-Learning: An International Journal, 8*(2), 372-386.

Castaneda, D. I., & Durán, W. F. (2018). Knowledge sharing in organizations: Roles of beliefs, training, and perceived organizational support. *Knowledge Management & E-Learning: An International Journal, 10*(2), 148-162.

CHEN, Z. J., Zhang, X. I., & Vogel, D. (2011). Exploring the Underlying Processes Between Conflict and Knowledge Sharing: A Work-Engagement Perspective 1. *Journal of applied social psychology, 41*(5), 1005-1033.

Cheung, M. W. (2007). Comparison of approaches to constructing confidence intervals for mediating effects using structural equation models. *Structural equation modeling: a multidisciplinary journal, 14*(2), 227-246.

Deci, E. L., & Ryan, R. M. (1980). The empirical exploration of intrinsic motivational processes. In *Advances in experimental social psychology* (Vol.

13, pp. 39-80). Academic Press.

Deci, E. L., & Ryan, R. M. (2000). The "what" and "why" of goal pursuits: Human needs and the self-determination of behavior. *Psychological inquiry, 11*(4), 227-268.

Davies, H., Leung, T. K., Luk, S. T., & Wong, Y. H. (1995). The benefits of "Guanxi": The value of relationships in developing the Chinese market. *Industrial marketing management, 24*(3), 207-214.

DeSimon, R. L., Werner, J. M., & Harris, D. M. (2002). Human Resource Development (3rd), Sea Harbod Drive.

Davenport, T. H., & Prusak, L. (1998). *Working knowledge: How organizations manage what they know.* Harvard Business Press.

Dawson, T. (2000). *Principles and practice of modern management.* Liverpool Academic Press.

DeSanctis G (1983) Expectancy theory as an explanation of voluntary use of a decision support system. *Psychological Reports 52*(1), 247-260.

De Spiegelaere, S., Van Gyes, G., & Van Hootegem, G. (2016). Not all autonomy is the same. Different dimensions of job autonomy and their relation to work engagement & innovative work behavior. *Human Factors and Ergonomics in Manufacturing & Service Industries, 26*(4), 515-527.

Emerson, R. (1976), Social exchange theory, *Annual Review of Sociology, 2*(1), 335-62.

Emde, R. J., Doherty, E. K., & Flynt, D. (2020). Relationships in online learning experiences: Identifying and creating positive relationships in online learning. In *Handbook of research on creating meaningful experiences in online courses* (pp. 140-152). IGI Global.

Easterby-Smith, M., Lyles, M. A., & Tsang, E. W. (2008). Inter-organizational knowledge transfer: Current themes and future prospects. *Journal of management studies, 45*(4), 677-690.

Flynn, F. J. (2003a). How much should I give and how often? The effects of generosity and frequency of favor exchange on social status and productivity. *Academy of Management Journal, 46*(5), 539-553.

Fornell, C., & Larcker, D. F. (1981). Evaluating structural equation models with unobservable variables and measurement error. *Journal of marketing research, 18*(1), 39-50.

Fei, X. (1992). From the soil. In From the Soil. University of California Press.

Gefen, D., Karahanna, E., & Straub, D. W. (2003). Trust and TAM in online shopping: An integrated model. *MIS quarterly*, 51-90.

Gupta, A. K., & Govindarajan, V. (2000). Knowledge management's social dimension: Lessons from Nucor Steel. *Sloan Management Review, 42*(1), 71-80.

Grant, R. M. (1991). The resource-based theory of competitive advantage: implications for strategy formulation. *California management review, 33*(3), 114-135.

Grant, R. M. (1996). Toward a knowledge-based theory of the firm. *Strategic management journal, 17*(S2), 109-122.

George, D., & Mallery, P. (1999). SPSS for windows step by step: a simple guide and reference. *Contemporary Psychology, 44*, 100-100.

Gao, H., Knight, J. G., Yang, Z., & Ballantyne, D. (2014). Toward a gatekeeping perspective of insider–outsider relationship development in China. *Journal of World Business, 49*(3), 312-320.

Husain, S. N., & Husain, Y. S. (2016). Mediating effect of OCB on relationship between job attitudes and knowledge sharing behavior. *International Journal of Science and Research (IJSR), 5*(1), 1008-1015.

Hung, S. Y., Lai, H. M., & Chang, W. W. (2011). Knowledge-sharing motivations affecting R&D employees' acceptance of electronic knowledge repository. *Behavior & Information Technology, 30*(2), 213-230.

Hendriks, P. (1999). Why share knowledge? The influence of ICT on the motivation for knowledge sharing. *Knowledge and process management, 6*(2), 91-100.

Hwang, K. K. (1987). Face and favor: The Chinese power game. *American journal of Sociology, 92*(4), 944-974.

Hau, Y. S., Kim, B., Lee, H., & Kim, Y. G. (2013). The effects of individual motivations and social capital on employees' tacit and explicit knowledge sharing intentions. *International Journal of Information Management, 33*(2), 356-366.

Heath, A. (1976). *Rational choice and social exchange: A critique of exchange theory.* CUP Archive.

Hatala, J. P. (2006). Social network analysis in human resource development: A new methodology. *Human Resource Development Review, 5*(1), 45-71.

Hansen, M. T. (2002). Knowledge networks: Explaining effective knowledge sharing in multiunit companies. *Organization science, 13*(3), 232-248.

Hwang, E. H., Singh, P. V., & Argote, L. (2015). Knowledge sharing in online communities: Learning to cross geographic and hierarchical boundaries. *Organization Science, 26*(6), 1593-1611.

Huber, G. P. (2001). Transfer of knowledge in knowledge management systems: unexplored issues and suggested studies. *European Journal of Information Systems, 10*(2), 72-79.

Hair, J. F., William C. B., Babin, B. J., & Anderson, R. E. (2010). *Multivariate Data Analysis.* Englewood Cliffs, NJ: Prentice Hall.

Hsu, M. H., Ju, T. L., Yen, C. H., & Chang, C. M. (2007). Knowledge sharing behavior in virtual communities: The relationship between trust, self-efficacy, and outcome expectations. *International journal of human-computer studies, 65*(2), 153-169.

Heisig, P. (2009). Harmonisation of knowledge management–comparing 160 KM frameworks around the globe. *Journal of knowledge management.*

Hult, G. T. M., Snow, C. C., and Kandemir, D. (2003). The role of entrepreneurship in building

cultural competitiveness in different organizational types. *Journal of Management, 29*(3), 401-426.

Hayes, A. F. (2009). Beyond Baron and Kenny: Statistical mediation analysis in the new millennium. *Communication monographs, 76*(4), 408-420.

Hitt, M. A., Lee, H. U., & Yucel, E. (2002). The importance of social capital to the management of multinational enterprises: Relational networks among Asian and Western firms. *Asia pacific journal of Management, 19*(2), 353-372.

Islam, T., Anwar, F., Khan, S. U. R., Rasli, A., Ahmad, U. N. B. U., & Ahmed, I. (2012). Investigating the mediating role of organizational citizenship behavior between organizational learning culture and knowledge sharing. *World Applied Sciences Journal, 19*(6), 795-799.

Ipe, M. (2003). Knowledge sharing in organizations: A conceptual framework.

Human resource development review, 2(4), 337-359.

Isaac, R. G., Zerbe, W. J., & Pitt, D. C. (2001). Leadership and motivation: The effective application of expectancy theory. *Journal of managerial issues*, 212-226.

Imlawi, J., & Gregg, D. (2020). Understanding the satisfaction and continuance intention of knowledge contribution by health professionals in online health communities. *Informatics for Health and Social Care, 45*(2), 151-167.

Jarvenpaa, S. L., & Staples, D. S. (2001). Exploring perceptions of organizational ownership of information and expertise. *Journal of management information systems, 18*(1), 151-183.

Janz, B. D., & Prasarnphanich, P. (2003). Understanding the antecedents of effective knowledge management: The importance of a knowledge-centered culture. *Decision sciences, 34*(2), 351-384.

Kahn, W. A. (1990). Psychological conditions of personal engagement and disengagement at work. *Academy of management journal, 33*(4), 692-724.

Kreitner, R. & Kinicki, A. (2007). Organizational Behavior. Boston: Mc-Graw-Hill.

Kotter, J. P. (1976). The psychological contract. *California Management review, XV* (3), 91-99.

Kim, H. S. (2017). A Study on Service Industry Development Policy by Service Nature. *Journal of Service Research and Studies, 7*(1), 15-26.

Kim, H. S. & Kim, S. J. (2015). The Effects of Individuality and Relationship of New Employee on Organizational Commitment and Job Satisfaction. *Journal of Practical Engineering Education, 7*(1), 39-45.

Kim, D. J., Ferrin, D. L., & Rao, H. R. (2008). A trust-based consumer decision-making model in electronic commerce: The role of trust, perceived risk, and their antecedents. *Decision Support Systems, 44*, 544-564.

Kim, S. J., & Park, M. (2015). Leadership, Knowledge Sharing, and Creativity. *The Journal of Nursing Administration, 45*(12), 615-621.

Kuok, A. C., & Taormina, R. J. (2017). Work engagement: Evolution of the concept and a new inventory. *Psychological Thought, 10*(2), 262-287.

Kirchner, K., Razmerita, L., & Sudzina, F. (2009). New forms of interaction and knowledge sharing on Web 2.0. In *Web 2.0* (pp. 1-16). Springer, Boston, MA.

Kim, W., Park, C. H., Song, J. H., & Yoon, S. W. (2012). Building a systematic model of employee engagement: The implications to research in human resource development. In *2012 Conference Proceedings of the Academy of Human Resource Development* (pp. 3916-3949). St. Paul, MN: The Academy of Human Resource Development.

Khanam, L., & Parveen, F. (2019). The Effects of Organizational Climate and Anticipated Reciprocal Relationship on Knowledge Sharing Behavior among Business Students in Bangladesh. *Institute of Business Administration (IBA-JU) Jahangirnagar University, 20*, 53.

Levene, H. (1961). Robust tests for equality of variances. Contributions to probability and statistics. *Essays in honor of Harold Hotelling*, 279-292.

Lu, F. C., & Zhou, P. (2006). Enterprise Network is an Efficient Organizational form for Cooperative Innovation. *Contemporary Finance & Economics, 262*, 53-57.

Lu, H. L. and Li, G. H. (2013). "Study on the Relationship of Organizational

Climate of Buying Center, Cross-Functional Knowledge Transfer and Procurement Performance." *Journal of Guizhou University Finance and Economics, 31*(2), 47-54.

Lai, S. C., & Tong, C. (2010). The Mediating Effect of Incentive and Reward System on the Relationship between Enterprise Ownership and Knowledge Sharing in Electronic Industry in Southern China. *International Journal of Interdisciplinary Social Sciences, 5*(5).

Luo, Y., Huang, Y., & Wang, S. L. (2012). Guanxi and organizational performance: A meta-analysis. *Management and Organization Review, 8*(1), 139-172.

Lauring, J. (2009). Managing cultural diversity and the process of knowledge sharing: A case from Denmark. *Scandinavian journal of management, 25*(4), 385-394.

Li, S., & Lin, B. (2006). Accessing information sharing and information quality in supply chain management. *Decision Support Systems, 42*(3), 1641-1656.

Liew, A. (2007). Understanding data, information, knowledge, and their inter-relationships. *Journal of knowledge management practice, 8*(2), 1-16.

Liu, H., Zhang, J., Liu, R., & Li, G. (2014). A model for consumer knowledge contribution behavior: the roles of host firm management practices, technology effectiveness, and social capital. *Information Technology and Management, 15*(4), 255-270.

Luo, Y. (1997). Guanxi and performance of foreign-invested enterprises in China: An empirical inquiry. *MIR: Management International Review*, 51-70.

Lin, T. C., & Huang, C. C. (2010). Withholding effort in knowledge contribution: The role of social exchange and social cognitive on project teams. *Information & Management, 47*(3), 188-196.

Li, X. (2011). Factors influencing the willingness to contribute information to online communities. *New Media & Society, 13*(2), 279-296.

Lin, M. J., Hung, S. W., & Chen, C. J. (2009). Fostering the determinants of knowledge sharing in professional virtual communities. *Computers in Human Behavior, 25*, 929-939.

Lee, W. H., Jang, H. J., & Noh, G. Y. (2020). Effects of user expectation relationship, self-esteem, and perceived pleasure on online video sharing. *Journal of Digital Contents Society, 21*(7), 1325-1334.

Li, Y. (2015). A Study on the Effects of Job Satisfaction and Organizational Commitment on Job Performance: A Study on Elementary and Middle School Teachers in China. Myongji University Graduate School Master's Thesis.

Moller, K., & Svahn, S. (2004). Crossing East-West boundaries: Knowledge sharing in intercultural business networks. *Industrial Marketing Management, 33*(3), 219-228.

Muthusamy, S. K., White, M. A., & Carr, A. (2007). An empirical examination of the role of social exchanges in alliance performance. *Journal of managerial issues*, 53-75.

Michailova, S., & Minbaeva, D. B. (2012). Organizational values and knowledge sharing in multinational corporations: *The Danisco case. International Business Review, 21*(1), 59-70.

Moberg, C. R., Cutler, B. D., Gross, A., & Speh, T. W. (2002). Identifying antecedents of information exchange within supply chains. *International Journal of Physical Distribution & Logistics Management.*

Ma, M., & Agarwal, R. (2007). Through a glass darkly: Information technology design, identity verification, and knowledge contribution in online communities. *Information systems research, 18*(1), 42-67.

Matschke, C., Moskaliuk, J., Bokhorst, F., Schümmer, T., & Cress, U. (2014). Motivational factors of information exchange in social information spaces. *Computers in Human Behavior, 36*, 549-558.

Mellor, S., Mathieu, J. E., Barnes-Farrell, J. L., & Rogelberg, S. G. (2001). Employees' nonwork obligations and organizational commitments: A new way to look at the relationships. *Human Resource Management: Published in Cooperation with the School of Business Administration, The University of Michigan and in alliance with the Society of Human Resources Management, 40*(2), 171-184.

Macey, W. H., & Schneider, B. (2008). The meaning of employee engagement. *Industrial and organizational Psychology, 1*(1), 3-30.

Mathibe, I. (2008). Expectancy theory and its implications for employee motivation. *Academic Leadership: The Online Journal, 6*(3), 8.

Millikan, R. G., & Woodfield, A. (1993). Knowing What I'm Thinking Of. *Proceedings of the Aristotelian Society, Supplementary Volumes, 67*, 91-124.

Macho, S., & Ledermann, T. (2011). Estimating, Testing, and Comparing Specific Effects in Structural Equation Models: The Phantom Model Approach. *Psychological Methods, 16*(1), 34-43.

Nadri, M., Hammouri, H., & Astorga, C. (2004). Observer design for continuous-discrete time state affine systems up to output injection. *European journal of control, 10*(3), 252-263.

Newell, S., Scarbrough, H., & Swan, J. (2009). *Managing knowledge work and innovation*. Bloomsbury Publishing.

Nonaka, I., & Konno, N. (1998). The concept of "Ba": Building a foundation for knowledge creation. *California management review, 40*(3), 40-54.

Noh, S., & Kang, B. (2021). A comparative study of motivations on social media platforms users' information sharing between South Korea and China. *The Journal of Internet Electronic Commerce Research, 21*(3), 187-202.

Noh, S., Zhao, L., & Kang, B. (2022). Information Sharing Intention in a Social Media Platform: A Study of Participants in the Chinese WeChat Moments. *Information Systems Review, 24*(1), 89-104.

Noh, S. (2021). Why do We Share Information? Explaining Information Sharing Behavior through a New Conceptual Model between Sharer to Receiver within SNS. *Asia Pacific Journal of Information Systems, 31*(3), 392-414.

O'Reilly, C., & Pondy, L. (1980). Organizational communications. In S. Kerr (Ed.), Organizational behavior (119-150). Columbus: Grid.

Organ, D. W., & Konovsky, M. (1989). Cognitive versus affective determinants of organizational citizenship behavior. *Journal of applied psychology, 74*(1), 157.

Ordonez de Pablos, P. (2005). "Western and Eastern Views on Social Networks." *The Learning Organization, 12*(5), 436-456

Passer, M. W., & Smith, R. E. (2004). *Psychology: The science of mind and behavior*. McGraw-Hill.

Porter, L. J., & Liebeskind, J. (1996). Knowledge, Strategy, and the Theory of the Firm. *Strategic Management Journal, 17*(S2), 93-107.

Parker, A., Cross, R., & Walsh, D. (2001). Improving collaboration with social network analysis: Leveraging knowledge in the informal organization. *Knowledge Management Review, 4,* 24-28.

Pavlou, P. A., & Fygenson, M. (2006). Understanding and predicting electronic commerce adoption: An extension of the theory of planned behavior. *MIS Quarterly, 30*(1), 115-143.

Park, M., & Moon, H. (2004). An empirical study on factors influencing knowledge sharing among groups. *Knowledge Management Research, 5*(2), 1-23.

Preacher, K. J., & Hayes, A. F. (2008). Asymptotic and resampling strategies for assessing and comparing indirect effects in multiple mediator models. *Behavior research methods, 40*(3), 879-891.

Ramasamy, M., & Thamaraiselvan, N. (2011). Knowledge sharing and organizational citizenship behavior. *Knowledge and Process Management, 18*(4), 278-284.

Razmerita, L., Phillips-Wren, G., & Jain, L. C. (2016). Advances in knowledge management: an overview. *Innovations in knowledge management,* 3-18.

Ray, S., Kim, S. S., & Morris, J. G. (2014). The central role of engagement in online communities. *Information Systems Research, 25*(3), 528-546.

Robinson, G. M. (1992). *Managing after the superlatives: Effective senior management development for the 1990's*. Tudor (Hodder & Stoughton).

Ryu, S., Ho, S. H., & Han, I. (2003). Knowledge sharing behavior of physicians in hospitals. *Expert Systems with applications, 25*(1), 113-122.

Ruggles, R. (1998). The state of the notion: knowledge management in practice. *California management review, 40*(3), 80-89.

Radaelli, G., Lettieri, E., Mura, M., & Spiller, N. (2014). Knowledge sharing and innovative work behavior in healthcare: A micro-level investigation of direct and indirect effects. *Creativity and Innovation Management, 23*(4), 400-414.

Rich, B. L., Lepine, J. A., & Crawford, E. R. (2010). Job engagement: Antecedents and effects on job performance. *Academy of management journal, 53*(3), 617-635.

Raban, D. R., and Rafaeli, S. (2007). Investigating ownership and the willingness to share information online. *Computers in Human Behavior, 23*(5), 2367-2382.

Snead, K. C., & Harrell, A. M. (1994). An application of expectancy theory to explain a manager's intention to use a decision support system. *Decision Sciences, 25*(4), 499-510.

Sinkula, J. M. (1994). Market information processing and organization learning. *Journal of Marketing, 58*, 35-45.

Spender, J. C. (1996). Making knowledge the basis of a dynamic theory of the firm. *Strategic management journal, 17*(S2), 45-62.

Song, J. H., Kim, W., Chai, D. S., & Bae, S. H. (2014). The impact of an innovative school climate on teachers' knowledge creation activities in Korean schools: The mediating role of teachers' knowledge sharing and work engagement. *KEDI Journal of Educational Policy, 11*(2).

Schein, E. H. (1980). Organizational psychology. New Jersey: Prentice-Hall.

Shuck, B., & Wollard, K. (2010). Employee engagement and HRD: A seminal review of the foundations. *Human resource development review, 9*(1), 89-110.

Sparrowe, R. T., & Liden, R. C. (1997). Process and structure in leader-member exchange. *Academy of management Review, 22*(2), 522-552.

Schaufeli, W. B., Salanova, M., González-Romá, V., & Bakker, A. B. (2002). The measurement of engagement and burnout: A two sample confirmatory factor analytic approach. *Journal of Happiness studies, 3*(1), 71-92.

Saks, A. M. (2006). Antecedents and consequences of employee engagement. Journal of managerial psychology.

Sair, S. A., & Danish, R. Q. (2018). Effect of performance expectancy and effort expectancy on the mobile commerce adoption intention through personal innovativeness among Pakistani consumers. *Pakistan Journal of Commerce and social sciences (PJCSS), 12*(2), 501-520.

Sun, H. (2012). Knowledge sharing, job attitudes and ehaviorional citizenship ehavior. *Industrial Management and Data Systems, 112*(1), 64-82.

Teh, P. L., & Yong, C. C. (2011). Knowledge sharing in IS personnel: Organizational behavior's perspective. *Journal of Computer Information Systems, 51*(4), 11-21.

Triandis, H. C. (1979). Values, attitudes, and interpersonal behavior. In *Nebraska symposium on motivation*. University of Nebraska Press.

Teece, D. J. (2000). Managing intellectual capital. New York: Oxford University Press.

Tsang, E. W. (1998). Can guanxi be a source of sustained competitive advantage for doing business in China? *Academy of Management Perspectives, 12*(2), 64-73.

Tang, P. M., Bavik, Y. L., Chen, Y. F., & Tjosvold, D. (2015). Linking ethical leadership to knowledge sharing and knowledge hiding: The mediating role of psychological engagement. *International Proceedings of Economics Development and Research, 84*, 71-76.

Vithessonthi, C. (2008). Social interaction and knowledge sharing behaviors in multinational corporations. *The Business Review, 10*(2), 324-331.

Vuori, V., & Okkonen, J. (2012). Knowledge sharing motivational factors of using an intra-organizational social media platform. *Journal of knowledge management, 16*(4), 592-603.

Van Dyk, P. S. (2002). *Definition of scope of human resources management.* In: Nel, P.S.

Venkatesh, V., Morris, M. G., Davis, G. B., & Davis, F. D. (2003). User acceptance of information technology: Toward a unified view. *MIS quarterly*, 425-478.

Venkatesh, V., Thong, J. Y., & Xu, X. (2012). Consumer acceptance and use of information technology: extending the unified theory of acceptance and use of technology. *MIS quarterly*, 157-178.

Venkatesh, V., & Davis, F. D. (2000). A theoretical extension of the technology acceptance model: Four longitudinal field studies. *Management science, 46*(2), 186-204.

Vroom, V. H. (1964). Work and Motivation. New York: Wiley.

Wang, W. T., & Hou, Y. P. (2015). Motivations of employees' knowledge sharing behaviors: A self-determination perspective. *Information and Or-*

ganization, 25(1), 1-26.

Wagner, C. (2006). Breaking the knowledge acquisition bottleneck through conversational knowledge management. *Information Resources Management Journal, 19*(1), 70-83.

Wang, S., & Noe, R. A. (2010). Knowledge sharing: A review and directions for future research. *Human resource management review, 20*(2), 115-131.

Wang, S., Noe, R. A., & Wang, Z. M. (2014). Motivating knowledge sharing in knowledge management systems: A quasi–field experiment. *Journal of Management, 40*(4), 978-1009.

Wasko, M. M., & Faraj, S. (2005). Why should I share? Examining social capital and knowledge contribution in electronic networks of practice. *MIS quarterly*, 35-57.

Wellman, B. & Frank, K. A. (2001). "Network capital in a multilevel world: getting support from personal communities." In *Lin, N. & Burt, R. S. & Cook, K. (eds.), Social Capital*, 233-273. Hawthorne: Aldine De Gruyter.

Wang, S., & Noe, R. A. (2010). Knowledge sharing: A review and directions for future research. *Human resource management review, 20*(2), 115-131.

Williams, J., & MacKinnon, D. P. (2008). Resampling and distribution of the product methods for testing indirect effects in complex models. *Structural equation modeling: a multidisciplinary journal, 15*(1), 23-51.

Yu, C. P., & Chu, T. H. (2007). Exploring knowledge contribution from an OCB perspective. *Information & management, 44*(3), 321-331.

Yoo, Y., & Torrey, B. (2002). National culture and knowledge management in a global learning organization. *The strategic management of intellectual capital and organizational knowledge, 421*, 454.

Yeung, I. Y., & Tung, R. L. (1996). Achieving business success in Confucian societies: The importance of guanxi (connections). *Organizational dynamics, 25*(2), 54-65.

Yu, C., Yu, T. F., & Yu, C. C. (2013). Knowledge sharing, organizational climate, and innovative behavior: A cross-level analysis of effects. *Social Behavior and Personality: an international journal, 41*(1), 143-156.

Yuan, F., & Woodman, R. W. (2010). Innovative behavior in the workplace: The role of performance and image outcome expectations. *Academy of management journal, 53*(2), 323-342.

Appendix A.
China's SMEs Introduction

Small and medium-sized enterprises refer to enterprises established in accordance with the law within the territory of the People's Republic of China with relatively small staff and operating scales, including medium-sized enterprises, small enterprises, and micro-enterprises.

On June 18, 2011, the Ministry of Industry and Information Technology, the National Bureau of Statistics, the National Development and Reform Commission, and the Ministry of Finance jointly issued the "Notice on Issuing the Provisions on the Classification Standards for Small and Medium-sized Enterprises," which stipulated that the classification standards for various industries are:

(1) Agriculture, forestry, animal husbandry and fishery. Small, medium, and micro enterprises with operating income below 200 million yuan. Among them, those with an operating income of 5 million yuan and above are medium-sized enterprises, those with an operating income of 500,000 yuan and above are small enter-

prises, and those with an operating income of less than 500,000 yuan are micro-enterprises.

(2) Industry. Those with fewer than 1,000 employees or less than 4 million yuan in operating income are small, medium, and micro enterprises. Among them, 300 employees or more, and operating income of 20 million yuan or more are medium-sized enterprises; 20 employees or more, and operating income of 3 million yuan or more are small enterprises; employees fewer than 20 or operating income below 3 million yuan are micro-enterprises.

(3) Construction industry. Small, medium, and micro enterprises with operating income of less than 80 million yuan or total assets of less than 80,000 yuan. Among them, business income of 60 million yuan and above, and total assets of 50 million yuan and above are medium-sized enterprises; business income of 3 million yuan and above, and total assets of 3 million yuan and above are small enterprises; operating income of 3 million yuan or less or micro-enterprises with total assets of less than 3 million yuan.

(4) Wholesale industry. Those with fewer than 200 employees or less than 4 million yuan in operating income are small, medium, and micro enterprises. Among them, those with 20 or more employees and operating income of 50 million yuan or more are medium-sized enterprises; those with 5 or more employees and operating income of 10 million yuan or more are small enterprises;

and those with fewer than 5 employees or operating income below 10 million yuan are micro-enterprises.

(5) Transportation industry. Those with fewer than 1,000 employees or less than 300 million yuan in operating income are small, medium, and micro enterprises. Among them, 300 employees or more, and operating income of 30 million yuan or more are medium-sized enterprises; 20 employees or more, and operating income of 2 million yuan or more are small enterprises; those with fewer than 20 employees or operating income below 2 million yuan are micro-enterprises.

(6) Retail industry. Those with fewer than 300 employees or less than 200 million yuan in operating income are small, medium, and micro enterprises. Among them, 50 employees or more, and operating income of 5 million yuan or more are medium-sized enterprises; 10 employees or more, and operating income of 1 million yuan or more are small enterprises; fewer than 10 employees or operating income below 1 million yuan are micro-enterprises.

(7) Accommodation industry and catering industry. Those with fewer than 300 employees or less than 100 million yuan in operating income are small, medium, and micro enterprises. Among them, those with 100 or more employees and operating income of 20 million yuan or more are medium-sized enterprises; those with 10 or more employees and operating income of 1 million yuan or more

are small enterprises; and those with fewer than 10 employees or operating income below 1 million yuan are micro-enterprises.

*(8) **Information transmission industry.** Those with fewer than 2,000 employees or less than 100 million yuan in operating income are small, medium, and micro enterprises.*

Note: Articles (6), (7), and (8) 3, those with 10 or more employees and operating income of 1 million yuan or more are small enterprises; those with fewer than 10 employees or operating income of 1 million yuan or less are micro-enterprises enterprise.

*(9) **Software and information technology service industry.** Those with fewer than 300 employees or less than 100 million yuan in operating income are small, medium, and micro enterprises. Among them, 100 employees or more, and operating income of 10 million yuan or more are medium-sized enterprises; 10 employees or more, and operating income of 500,000 yuan or more are small enterprises; fewer than 10 employees or operating income below 500,000 yuan are micro-enterprises.*

*(10) **Warehousing industry.** Those with fewer than 200 employees or less than 30 million yuan in operating income are small, medium, and micro enterprises.*

Note: Articles (8) (9) (10) 3, of which 100 employees and above, and operating income of 10 million yuan and above are medium-sized enterprises

(11) The postal industry. Medium-sized enterprises with operating income of 20 million yuan and above; Note: (10) (11) Article 2. Those with 20 employees or more and operating income of 1 million yuan or more are small enterprises; those with 20 employees or less or operating income of 1 million yuan or less are micro-enterprises. Small, medium, and micro enterprises with fewer than 1,000 employees in the transportation and postal industries or with operating income of less than 300 million yuan. Among them, there are 300 employees and above.

(12) Real estate development and operation. Small, medium, and micro enterprises with operating income of less than 20 million yuan or total assets of less than 100 million yuan. Among them, business income of 10 million yuan and above, and total assets of 50 million yuan and above are medium-sized enterprises; business income of 1 million yuan and above, and total assets of 20 million yuan and above are small enterprises; operating income of 1 million yuan or less or micro-enterprises with total assets of less than 20 million yuan.

(13) Property management. Those with fewer than 1,000 employees or less than 50 million yuan in operating income are small, medium, and micro enterprises. Among them, 300 employees or more, and operating income of 10 million yuan or more are medium-sized enterprises; 100 employees or more, and operating

income of 5 million yuan or more are small enterprises; fewer than 100 employees or operating income below 5 million yuan are micro-enterprises.

(14) Leasing and business service industry. Those with fewer than 300 employees or total assets of less than 120 million yuan are small, medium, and micro enterprises. Among them, those with 100 employees or more and total assets of 80 million yuan or more are medium-sized enterprises; those with 10 or more employees and total assets of 1 million yuan or more are small enterprises; and those with less than 10 employees or total assets are small enterprises. Those with less than 1 million yuan are micro-enterprises.

(15) Other unspecified industries. Those with fewer than 300 employees are small, medium, and micro enterprises. Among them, those with 100 or more employees are medium-sized enterprises; those with 10 or more employees are small enterprises; and those with fewer than 10 employees are micro-enterprises.

Appendix B.
Geographical Distribution of
China's SMEs Samples

The sample enterprises are from twenty-three provinces, four special autonomous regions, and Hong Kong special region. The geographical distribution of the sample enterprises is concentrated in the southeast coastal provinces of China, such as Guangdong province, Zhejiang province, Jiangsu province, Shanghai city, etc. The geographical distribution reflects the distribution characteristics and regional characteristics of SMEs in China.

Taking Guangdong Province as an example, the geographical distribution of sample enterprises is concentrated in Shenzhen, Guangzhou, and other cities. It mainly reflects the distribution characteristics of SMEs in the big cities along the southeast coast.

*Data source tracking (n=531 follow-up samples)

Figure 9-1. Geographical Distribution of China's SMEs Sample

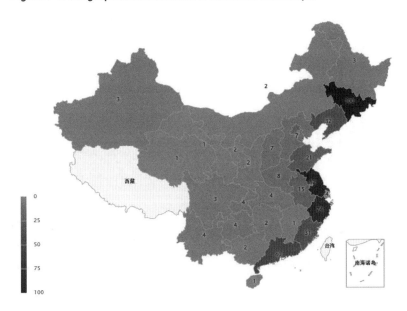

Figure 9-2. Geographical Distribution of China's SMEs Sample

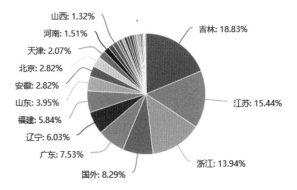

Figure 9-3. Geographical Distribution of China's SMEs Sample

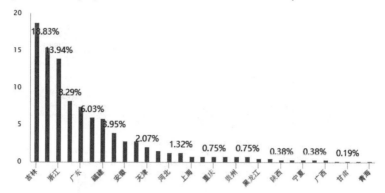